AF412539

THE LIGHT OF KRISHNAMURTI

By

Gabriele Blackburn

Published in 1996 by: IDYLWILD BOOKS
P.O. BOX 246
OJAI VALLEY
CA. 93024-0246

Library of Congress Catalog Card Number: 96-94645

ISBN: 0-9613054-4-4

Cover Design by Fred Colcer
Interior Design and Production: Ojai Valley Graphic Ink

Manufactured in the United States of America

First Printing 1996

PHOTOGRAPHS

FRONT COVER: Studio Enhancement signed and given by Krishnamurti to James Vigeveno, 1927.

FRONTISPIECE: Photo from a film taken of Krishnamurti by Albert Blackburn, 1949.

	Page
Rajagopal, Krishnamurti, Annie Besant, 1929.	2
Our "Hut" at Ommen Star Camp.	16
The author blowing bubbles.	20
The Campfire; and seated: José Vigeveno, Rajagopal, Annie Besant and Krishnamurti.	21
James and Annie Vigeveno, 1945.	32
Krishnamurti, 1948.	48
The author, 1949.	68
Al and Gabie Blackburn, 1976.	112
Al Blackburn, 1981.	134
Krishnamurti greeting Al Blackburn.	152
Author with her Lhasa Apso puppies.	166

CONTENTS:

AUTHOR'S NOTE

PAGE

1. The Light Without Shadow   1
2. The Light of Truth   15
3. The Light of Beauty   31
4. The Light of Bliss   47
5. From Darkness to Light   67
6. The Light that Resolves   95
7. The Light of Observation   111
8. The Light of the World   133
9. The Light of Clarity   151
10. The Light to Oneself   165

APPENDIX - POEMS: 175
EXPRESSIONS OF LOVE

  First Attempts   179
  Thoughts of Devotion   191
  Listening to Myself   199

  The State of Love   225

ORDER FORMS

AUTHOR'S NOTE

This book flowered out of my life which has been so marvelously inspired by the extraordinary presence of J. Krishnamurti. I was born into a family who worked with him, and I was raised with his teachings. Krishnaji was my friend. I will describe the effect he had on my life - although my life would be of little importance, were it not a testimony to the tremendous value of his teachings.

It has been impressed on me, by what Krishnaji called, the "eternal Light," that it is important to relate the mystical events which I saw and experienced, as they were a unique part of our relationship. I will describe them exactly as they occurred, without embellishment, or interpretation.

Perhaps this story will shed some Light upon the life of Krishnamurti, this eternal Being.

Ojai, California 1996

1

THE LIGHT
WITHOUT SHADOW

*There was light without shadow
and it was Light.*

KRISHNAMURTI'S NOTEBOOK   1961

My mother, Annie Stern was German, and raised in a Jewish family. She was sensitive, an accomplished pianist, and had a sharp intellect which balanced her nature. She earned her Ph.D. in Psychology at the University of Frankfurt, and did her post-graduate work assisting in some famous experiments.

Her family thought she should marry and settle down, and asked a business associate, also Jewish, from the Netherlands about his sons. He suggested Dr. José Vigeveno, who was an ambassador, the head of the Red Cross, and also the head of the Theosophical Society in Holland. But they were not attracted to each other.

However, his brother James fell in love with Annie's beauty. James was a very sensitive, and intuitive man, with a passion for life, and great charisma which swept Annie off her feet. He was a well-known character actor who traveled all over Europe giving performances of classical and modern plays. At that time, this was not considered to be an "honorable" profession, and so he was persuaded to join the family business in order for the couple to be married. This business, the manufacturing of fine cloth, woolens, and coats was also established in Holland, England and Europe. They lived near

Berlin in a lovely home given to them at their wedding. They had a son, Henk and then a daughter, Sylvia.

José told them of the coming of the world teacher, believed by the Theosophists to be J. Krishnamurti, and in 1927 and 1928 they attended the Star Camp meetings in Ommen, Holland. They never felt inclined to join "The Order of the Star of the East" but were interested in hearing what was to be brought as a great truth of life.

In 1929, they again traveled to Ommen to listen to Krishnamurti. On the third of that August, Krishnamurti made his extraordinary exclamation of dissolving the entire organization of "The Order of the Star" that had been set up for him, and stated that, "Truth is a pathless land." They immediately felt the immensity of that truth, and realized that they wished to live their lives in that freedom.

They told Krishnamurti how they felt, and offered him their help and support. This was the beginning of their more than 40 years of work for him. It started by Annie opening the first office in Berlin to spread his teachings. She also translated many of his books into German, and I have been told that they are excellent. They worked closely with him in Holland, and later in America.

The exuberance, joy and high energy of those days

also inspired them to consciously ask for a third child. They wished for one who would be able to understand the immensity of Krishnamurti's teachings, live them, and be a bearer of that Light of Truth. Apparently such a one was attracted to them, as I was conceived in Ommen that summer.

I was born on May 10, 1930, a date so close to Krishnamurti's birth date that they took it as a sign. As it turned out, my brother and sister were never very interested in the teachings and went their own way, even though they had the exact same environment and upbringing.

❧

My mother said that I was a good baby and gave no one trouble, that I seemed perfectly content to stare in wonder at everything. I was very, very shy, and that shyness has continued.

When I didn't speak clearly at 2 1/2 years, they wondered if it was because both the German and Dutch languages were spoken to us, but they discovered that my tongue was tied down too close to the tip. I remember sensing very strongly that something was wrong when one day we went somewhere and my mother did not feel comfortable holding me. She was not herself somehow, and seemed to be hiding something. It was as if she didn't really want to hold me. I had never felt her like that.

And then a doctor said, "Open your mouth and I'll give you a candy" - which he did - but only after cutting under my tongue and causing great pain and shock. There was no enjoyment of the sweet mixed with blood. I don't think I have ever quite trusted doctors again, but a capacity to feel when people were not speaking the truth has always remained very strong in me. It has nothing to do with logical thinking.

I only remember our home in Germany from the viewpoint of sitting happily at the bottom of a slope, on a very large lawn leading up to a very large house. I loved that lawn, and loved playing on it. I was always the happiest when I could play outside because the world seemed so much more real to me.

When I was 3 years old, Hitler came to power. There was a fearful incident thrust on my brother of being rolled in a garbage can. The atmosphere was getting very dangerous for people of the Jewish race. My parents decided to leave, and move everything to Holland.

There was some danger on the train trip, and I felt great tension from my mother who feared we might be stopped. But we got across the border safely, though she carried jewelry and cash with her.

We spoke only Dutch from then on, and although the language came easily enough, I noticed that I had a mistrust of words. I always felt very strongly about everything. But when I tried to express things, the words were never adequate to convey the reality of the feeling. This caused uncomfortable reactions and impatience in most people, but both my parents seemed to understand it to some degree.

My father also had no patience for endless words, too much logical thinking, or any intellectual exercises. He could always sense the situation, feel it out in a quiet way within himself, and go right to the crux of the matter pointing out the important thing involved. This was a wonderful talent, which I appreciated immensely when I was able to fully understand the significance of living that way.

My mother took more care, and would think things through more thoroughly. When she saw I had trouble finding words, she would patiently teach me similar words to consider. As I grew older she would suggest words, but let me make my own decisions as to which were the most accurate for me. I admired her for this capacity to search for the most meaningful words. However, I still feel that words are very weak indicators of the actual.

My mother said that it was never hard to put me in bed to go to sleep. On the contrary, I often asked to go, for I loved it! No one ever knew why, for I felt instinctively that they wouldn't know what I was talking about. No one from my family was ever in my sleep-world.

When I fell asleep, I went into a whole different world, one which was magical, one which was made of pure Light and love. It was the familiar world from where I had come before I was born.

It was a world of children, fairies and magical beings. And it was a world of nice people who loved being there. It was a world full of incredible nature, always sunny - unlike cloudy, cold Holland. I could go wherever I wanted, whether into a meadow full of flowers, or a waterway, or sit in trees that were fantastic, or fly on a magical horse through the skies.

Anything was possible because it was not just a dreamland, not only play-time, not fantasy or imagination. It was a place of great reality of being; great reality of seeing, hearing, music, touching, smelling flowers, and participation in the love and joy of life itself.

There was a powerful energy that united me to
everything there. It was an actual experiencing state
of being. I could certainly distinguish dreams from
this place of being at one with everything.

And then, the most incredible part was that a great
Being of the most beautiful, brilliant Light was
always there, creating and maintaining that
wholeness of love, that feeling of immensity which I
just instinctively knew was the actual reality of all
life. It was a place of being whole, complete, happy,
where all went well, easily, where a sense of being
free was natural.

It was a world where there was no seeking without
finding; no feeling of inadequacy, pain or incapacity.
I felt that whatever I needed to be was here, and that
just being here was the most important thing to feel.
As a little child I was very curious, and that led me
to find out many things. But it was not necessary or
possible to bring back words of description into
wakefulness.

And, there were times when I was not a little child at
all, but a grown person with an inner understanding
of the greatness that was there. It was as if I already
had an innate knowing of what was important in life,
and that this state of being was the way to live.

At times, I would sit with many others and listen to that beautiful Great Light Being. I never saw his face as he was too brilliant, and one could not look directly at him. There was only the wholeness of listening. At the end of the talking, a wholeness of love would flood the valley where we sat, and fill me with a feeling so marvelous that I can only say it was a wholeness of being.

A shudder of energy would involuntarily shoot through me, as if lightning had passed through me. And then I would wake up.

There was nothing as beautiful as that in my wakeful life. School was a painful forcing of learning, being told to be unlike myself, conforming to a system of patterns of becoming what teachers were expecting me to be. And no one I knew was like those beings in my sleep-world. I could easily go back there, but that, of course, was not allowed in school; was thought of as day-dreaming and not paying attention to the lessons.

The only link from my sleep-world to my daily life was music. There was always music, mostly classical, in our home. Music was the only link that could connect me to that other reality beyond the words or the ideas of people. I would lie on the rug and listen for hours to music, and also be connected to that other sleep-world. The purity, simplicity and feeling of immensity of love was possible in the state of listening to music.

Whenever I listened completely to music, I would again touch that wholeness of being, and those same powerful shudders of energy would pass through me. I didn't understand them then, but I knew that it had absolutely nothing to do with my thinking self. It was not anything I could relate to consciously, so I just stopped trying to figure it out, and left it alone, as being some mysterious occurrence. After all, it made me feel wonderful.

So music became the most important, vital thing in my life - the one that had meaning beyond words. My mother played the piano beautifully. We had a Steinway grand piano, and it was always covered with a large oriental brocade cover which hung well over the sides. I used to sit under it while she played, and just listen to the fullness and echo of sounds. I kept little toys and treasures on the shelves underneath, which no one knew about.

So I created my own world of outer listening and inner being. Sometimes that wholeness of being would be touched, setting off the mysterious shudders of energy.

Much later in life, when I found my true work, these shudders of energy were made clear to me, and I finally found out what they were.

I started to learn to play the piano when I was about six years old. It never failed to both enthrall and delight me. Music became a great passion in my life, and I began to see myself as a musician.

2

THE LIGHT OF TRUTH

*That which is tremendously Light
has no shadow; it is clear.*

INDIA 1966

THE LIGHT OF TRUTH

When we moved to Holland we lived the first three years in Ommen. There were three "Huts", cottages, at the campground, and ours was the largest due to the large family. It was a very open, clear, white wood place with a porch, and room to play all around it.

The forest of small pines was all around, there was a lovely lake, and a fascinating deer park. I remember what fun we had when we were sent out to pick mushrooms; and also sometimes we found berries.

There was a little train on a short track which brought the food from the kitchen tent to the tables where the people ate. Of course we rode it whenever it was not being used. In the summers it was warm and beautiful, a delightful place for children, and I really blossomed there.

My love of being outdoors was nourished by that lovely place. At first I rode on the little back seat of a bicycle which our housekeeper/nanny rode on errands. Later on, when I could ride my own bicycle, the three of us children went everywhere around the extensive campground and woods.

The sense of being able to direct where I wanted to

ride was a marvelous thing. It began to bring me into the feeling of being able to be in charge of myself. I somehow made the connection of being free to direct the movements of my own life. This was terribly important because, as the youngest child I was told very often, by everyone, what to do.

There were many friends who visited my parents, and my uncle José and his family sometimes came by, as did other relatives.

But mostly we saw two gentlemen from India. They spoke another language, English, which we could not understand. One of them we called Raja - D. Rajagopal, Krishnamurti's secretary - who would sometimes bring his wife Rosalind and his little girl, Radha, who was a year younger than I, to play. He had little patience and hardly every looked at me. It seemed he was always talking, but there was no communication at all.

The other man whom Radha called "Krinsh," because she could not pronounce his name, was Krishnamurti. But somehow that didn't seem right for me, so I didn't call him anything. He was much more intense, yet it was so easy to run to him and hug. He was much more interested in looking at us children, and everything around us, and there was a spontaneous communication of feeling which didn't need words.

He was usually ushered around, and it seemed like he always had to be somewhere else. People seemed to need him, to ask him things all the time, and so they kept him busy.

But sometimes, Krishnaji would come and sit with us, and I remember his wonderful laughter which made me feel so wonderful, too. He watched what we did, how we played and always seemed very interested in whatever we were doing. Sometimes he would join us and walk about a little bit, and he would always point to things that interested him, as if showing us that it was important to look around us and notice everything.

I remember one occasion when I was blowing bubbles. I was always ready to cry when they broke and were gone. Somehow he conveyed by a little, "Oh," that it was enough to enjoy them, because they were so beautiful, and that it really didn't matter when they burst and were gone. I thought he meant because I could blow more bubbles, but then I saw that his joy in looking at them was enough for him. So I enjoyed looking at them, too, with him, and we laughed together when they burst. He had shown me the significance of being in the moment.

I also remember his touch or a loving hug when he picked me up, because it felt like it went right into me and filled me up with a wonderful feeling.

At night my parents went to the big campfires. They told us that there was chanting - we didn't know what that was - singing, poems and talks, but that it was for grownups only.

My brother was very curious and talked my sister and me into being very naughty and going to see the fire. We had seen the rows of logs for seats laid out in a large square around a clearing of a huge woodpile in the center. There were several chairs made of logs with high backs. We used to play there during the day when no one was around. So the temptation to go see such a big fire was tremendous. We got out of our beds, sneaked out of the house, and I walked with my heart thumping so loudly that I thought everyone there would hear it and we would be found out.

When we saw the campfire, it was the most beautiful thing with sparks flying up, and the sing-song of the chanting enthralled me. It stirred some distant feeling of something, but I couldn't remember what it was. There sitting in the special seats was uncle José - with his black beard glistening, the lady with white hair we knew - Annie Besant - Raja,

Krishnamurti and some other men. I almost ran to my uncle but my brother and sister stopped me in time.

We stayed a very long time it seems, as no one was looking in our direction. I don't think my parents ever found out that we saw it - my brother said that we shouldn't tell.

But the next time I saw Krishnaji, I knew he knew, but that he also knew that I knew he knew. But the wonderful thing was that it was all right with him. This was such a great relief to me. And that was the first time that I realized that he did not make a problem out of something.

However, I never again disobeyed my parents as I didn't want to ever feel that scared again. Not that they would have spanked us or anything, but there was a sense of what is right and wrong, and I thought we had done something wrong even though it was fascinating and felt so good. I don't remember how old I was, because although we were living in Aardenhout between Amsterdam and Zandvoort, we went to the Ommen camps every summer through 1938.

Our parents had this enormous love and concern for us children, and were interested in helping us find our own way. They always made a point of treating us exactly the same; if one got something, the others would also. This was to discourage competition, so that we did not feel left out.

But we were raised very differently from most children who are so heavily conditioned in their environmental culture. We were not taught Theosophy, the Jewish or any other organized religion. We were not taught that being Dutch was any better than any other nationality. We were not told to join groups or that any one tradition, people, or way of life was better than another.

On the contrary, my parents taught us how religions and nationalism divide people, how it causes competition between people who want to defend their way of life, and how all of that is the root of violence and creates conflict and wars.

We were often shown that just being different from another did not mean that we were any better or they any lesser. In this way, judgment of others was discouraged. In our home, we met people from all over the world, and all were welcomed equally and enthusiastically as a wonderful way to find out about others and their way of life.

In other words, we were raised according to the teachings of Krishnamurti. As a result of this non-conditioning into strong religious or other patterns, I did not have to struggle to free myself of crippling belief systems and prejudices. It was a tremendous way to raise children, and was the basis of Krishnamurti's views of true education.

We were always asked about what we felt and thought, and as we grew older, what we wanted to do in situations that came up. I always felt that I was listened to. My parents would point out the positive and negative consequences involved and what might happen if we went a certain way, made a certain decision, took a certain course. But having done that, when we were old enough, decisions concerning our life were always left to us.

So I made my own mistakes, learned my own lessons, and was given the confidence that somehow I could manage my own life. This became extremely important, since I put myself in many serious difficulties.

My parents stayed together their entire lives, always willing to listen, discuss and point out their opinions and feeling about any questions I might bring to them, remaining always a strong, loving support to me.

Krishnaji told Raja and my parents that a world war was brewing, and that we should all leave Holland and go to the United States, to continue the work there. My father understood the urgency and began to plan for the move.

They were excited about it all, and my father decided to change his profession and be an art dealer, as he had always wanted to have an art gallery. With this in mind he made the preparations for immigrating, transferred monies, and bought a lot of old Dutch paintings with which to begin the gallery.

They went to our hut in Ommen and cleared it out. On the way back, they decided to take a break from driving the car, and stopped in a small town to stretch their legs. When they saw a fortune-teller's sign - although they had never done such a thing before - on a whim they decided to go in. A voice from behind a curtain asked them to please wait a moment, but not to speak. When they went in, the lady there exclaimed in amazement that she had many things to tell them, one of which was of the utmost importance.

She gained their confidence by telling them that they were about to embark on a new life across the ocean, one that carried forward not only all that they had worked for, but which was of a deep spiritual

significance to them. She told them that they were
to continue to help in a work of the greatest
importance, and that their new life and profession
would be highly successful.

However, she said that there were some serious
obstacles in the later years, and that they must watch
out for them, because they would affect not only
them, personally. She also told them that they had
already overcome many problems through their own
wisdom, by moving to Holland, and also through
their work during the past nine years.

She said many other things of a more personal
nature which impressed them, as they were true, so
that when she came to the matter which she had
mentioned first as being of the utmost importance,
they were deeply moved. This matter was a serious
warning. She urged them not to delay their journey,
and not to take the ship, "The Amsterdam," on which
we were already booked. She insisted that they must
take an earlier ship as soon as possible. They
thanked her and left in amazement.

They decided to do as she had urged, feeling that her
insistence just might have some basis, and hastened
to change their plans. This meant rushing many
things, but they worked it out, and we left Holland
on "The Rotterdam" in the winter of 1939.

The journey lasted a miserable ten days as there were storms and I was ill the whole time. The ship was in blackout while torpedo boats chased us. However, we made it safely to New York. This was the last ship to make it. Soon after, "The Amsterdam" was sunk and there were no survivors.

3

THE LIGHT
OF BEAUTY

When there is great beauty like a mountain,
the majesty of it, the shade, the Light,
'you' don't exist.
The beauty of that thing
drives away the 'you'.

THE WAY OF INTELLIGENCE   1978

THE LIGHT OF BEAUTY

My first impression, from the ship, of the gigantic
Statue of Liberty was confusing. I couldn't figure
out how she could stand on top of the water.

As we went through the immigration process on
Ellis Island, I again sensed some fear from my
mother. Because I had been ill so much in my life,
and on the boat, the authorities thought I might have
pneumonia or tuberculosis.

We didn't have some medical papers, and a doctor
had to check us. It seemed a long wait, but finally
we were allowed to go through. Since then, I have
gone through many borders in my life, and each time
there is a little apprehension, especially if a bribe is
expected, as one is totally at the mercy of the
authorities.

New York was absolutely overwhelming. All the
buildings were so high that I could hardly find the
sky, and there seemed to be no land, only buildings
and roads. The one exception was Central Park,
which we went to once in a while, and I loved that
because it was a natural place. The top of the
Empire State building was fascinating, but a bit
scary as I wondered what held it up. Our hotel
room was very high up, too, so that the little cars

looked like toys, and you could hardly make out what the people looked like.

We spent long hours in those rooms while my parents visited the current art galleries and made contacts with the art dealers. Once we scared ourselves imagining what would happen if our parents didn't come back. I felt very isolated, and was so very happy to leave.

My parents bought a new four-door Ford and we drove off, taking the Southern route to Los Angeles. Although my father had graciously taken another Jewish boy my brother's age with us on the ship, and also a young lady to teach us English, we still knew none of the strange language which we heard all around us, as she had spoken German with us.

Some first impressions of new things were of the large size of the roads and countryside. It seemed this was a very large country, so expansive, and sometimes no houses or people were around, which made me wonder where they all were. Certainly they were not riding their bicycles, as we never saw any at all, which made me wonder if everybody had a car.

Also, there were the first black people we had seen.

They walked to the fields to work. In the towns they seemed to smile a lot, looking very friendly, and in the evenings they would sit on their porches to rest.

Another thing that was new were the billboards with the large pictures on them. They weren't very pretty, but you couldn't help seeing them. They advertised Coca Cola a lot, and this became a joke so that every time we saw one, we did a little "Volga Boat Song," singing, Coca Cola - uh! We tried some, of course, but I didn't like the stuff. I especially disliked carbonated drinks as they wouldn't stay down in my stomach, and didn't help the car sickness at all.

By the time we got to California, the only English words I had learned were: "yes," "no," and the phrase "The sky is blue and the trees are green" — unless you want to count "Coca Cola." There was too much for the family to see and talk about, so lessons did not flourish.

When we got to Los Angeles we couldn't find it. Nobody was sure where we were. It seemed to go on and on - and then we were at the Pacific Ocean. We all got out and walked on the beach, celebrating our arrival. Having looked at the maps the whole 3,000 miles, to have gone from shore to shore was for us a tremendous achievement and joy.

We continued on and drove to Ojai Valley in order to connect with Krishnaji, Raja and Rosalind. Arya Vihara, their home, was beautiful. It had lovely trees, lawns and flowers, and we could walk right through the wonderful orange trees. We received a very warm welcome. Krishnaji was so relaxed and went around with a twinkle in his eye, showing us everything. I immediately felt at home there.

The three of us children were put in a boarding school, the Ojai Valley School - for a semester, in order to learn English.

My parents went to San Francisco to check it out, but decided on Los Angeles. They bought a lovely home being built on a hill in Westwood, near Bel Air. They added a large gallery show room, a smaller individual show room, and an office with storage space. And, as they had to build something under it for support, they put a small apartment. Each of us children, as we started our married life, used it for a time.

My father wanted to show paintings as they would look in a home environment, a very unique idea for a gallery, and one which worked remarkably well. As their business grew, paintings, water colors, drawings and etchings all found their way into the entire house, storage basement, and upper bedrooms, as the children grew and left the home.

There was only one other art gallery in Los Angeles at the time, and all the Hollywood movie-makers started collecting art. The business was run entirely by my parents, and later with the help of a secretary. They alternated taking trips to Europe after the war to replenish the stock. It gained a high reputation, specializing in modern French art, and introducing many American artists.

When they could retire early, my father remaining a "gentleman Dealer," did special showings only at the Bel Air Hotel by private appointment, and clients also came to our home in Ojai.

But my parents made themselves more and more free to spend a great deal more time and money on the Krishnamurti work. The records, catalogues and photos of the James Vigeveno Gallery are in the Smithsonian Institution now.

When we first arrived in Ojai, I immediately fell in love with it: the lovely valley, the mountains all around wherever I looked - a constant wonder after flat Holland - the meadows and wild flowers to play in, the fruit trees, and the palms which I had never seen; the hills to climb - it all had such a sense of great balance. I really felt that I belonged in Ojai. That feeling never changed and I returned to Ojai every chance possible, finally settling here for good.

I am still always delighted by that special light just after sunset, which is called "The Pink Moment." As it spreads a glorious glow onto the mountains, the light is reflected throughout the valley in a profuse violet hue.

That magnificent light somehow enhances all the colors of everything in the valley, and I always sense a delicacy in the atmosphere as the day pauses and comes to a hush.

Within a year, my parents bought five acres above the Oak Grove where Krishnamurti spoke. It was a haven, with marvelous old oak trees surrounded by intriguing open spaces to walk and explore in. I really felt I had come home because it reminded me so much of my sleep-valley where all was so peaceful.

My parents immediately set out to build their retirement home, being sure to have a large living room so that Krishnaji could have discussions there, as there was none at Arya Vihara.

From then on, Krishnaji had fairly large groups of

people for discussions in both our homes, the beautiful Ojai one with its wide porches under the oak trees, overlooking the large lawns and gardens, and the large lovely gallery room which also overlooked beautiful gardens.

We learned English very fast - we had to for self-defense. There were some very spoiled children who relentlessly teased us, but luckily I had my brother and sister to protect me.

On my 10th birthday, May 10, 1940, the teachers dressed me up in a Dutch costume to celebrate. Suddenly the news came over the radio that Holland had been invaded by German paratroopers. It was a sad day of great worry for all our family and friends. Although we heard news from Europe during those terrible war years, we didn't realize the full extent of the horrors we were so lucky to have escaped until much later. When the war ended we had lost 32 members of our family.

In the fall we entered the public school system, attached to the University of California at Los Angeles - U.C.L.A. There were many young aspiring teachers, some who understood how strange we felt, and were very kind and helped us along. Within a year and a half we had lost our accents and were treated as equals by other children.

I was very shy, and only made friends cautiously, feeling akin to girls who were of an artistic nature, sensitive, and who wondered about the world. I never could find much in common with those girls who only wanted to be like everybody else, who cared more for outward looks, make-up, lipstick and nail polish - who seemed so superficial and only interested in themselves and how to attract boyfriends.

I think that being so close to the movie industry where looks were everything, and the fact that most girls dreamed of being discovered, had a great influence. I didn't get interested in boys until I was sixteen.

I never wanted to be like everybody else in order to be accepted, and always went my own way without feeling that I was missing out on anything. For example, when I discovered sandals, I never wanted to wear shoes, and began to wear sandals almost all the time, not caring what people thought. I still do.

Life was good, and whenever possible I went to Ojai with my mother or father. I spent most of my weekends and vacations there. Ojai became the focus of my life, a place which sustained and nourished that inner life of feeling-being of my sleep-world. I instinctively knew there was so much to learn and experience, yet I had no idea what that was, or what I really wanted.

I seemed to be living my life like a new flower bud, not knowing what type or color it would be. I had such a strong feeling that something very important was missing, and I always would feel inadequate until I knew what was to be my life's work.

Then, when I had just turned 14 years old, came one of the extraordinary mystical events of my life. On the night of May 13, 1944, I again entered that lovely sleep-valley and sat to listen to the wisdom of that Light Being. When he finished, and that wholeness of love entered me, I got up to leave and awaken as usual.

However, he motioned to me to wait. As he approached me, that brilliant Light radiated from him, and formed an exquisite oval all around him. For the first time, I could see his extraordinary face, one of such tremendous depth of wisdom, glorious beauty, and purity of love. It was the face of Krishnamurti! The familiar, kind gentleman I had known all my life, was actually this immense being!

I melted away - I didn't exist - only the reality of that Light Being existed. A feeling of complete awe came over me as I looked at him. I suddenly started to prostrate myself in front of him, but he stopped me. I felt a power that almost caused me to faint – which would have been waking up.

He spoke to calm me once again into myself, saying: "You know me, Gabie. Go to the Oak Grove tomorrow and listen. You will hear what you have been yearning for, and you will understand all of this. You will not need to come back here again, for now your inner work begins and we can communicate directly."

As I thanked him, a feeling of loving warmth penetrated my inner being. That now familiar involuntary shudder of pure energy passed through me. And I awoke with great expectancy into the day.

I rushed out into the garden of our Ojai home and hugged my horse. In haste, I brushed and cleaned her, fed and watered her. She had taken me all over the valley, by streams, through orchards, into the hills, giving me a wonderful feeling of freedom. I so much enjoyed being alone in movement, wondering at everything we encountered. Now she would take me into my new life.

I rushed back into the house, hardly daring to speak

to anyone, lest I lose what felt like a sacred trust. I
ate some fruit, put on my English riding clothes,
slipped a bridle over my horse's head, jumped on her
and rode down the hill, to get the movement of the
day started.

It was much too early, but I rode around the area
with a sense of great urgency. This was the first
time after the war that Krishnaji was to talk again. I
watched many people arrive, but didn't want to talk
to anyone. I felt as if all time was suspended
between his revelation, my waking up, and what I
would hear this morning.

I waited until I saw Krishnaji's car approach, and
only then rode up the path leading into the Oak
Grove. I rode past my father waiting to walk
Krishnaji in, tied my horse to a tree, waved to my
mother working at the book table, and walked in.

Krishnaji walked up next to me and looked at me
very intently for a long moment. Again, there was
that immediate understanding between us, this time
an affirmation of the important meeting of the
previous night. I realized that the direct
communication had begun. And indeed, I never
visited that sleep-valley again.

As he took his place and stood waiting for the
audience to be ready to listen, that radiance all

around him - a calming but vibrant energy radiated from him. His first words were:

"Amidst so much confusion and sorrow it is essential to find creative understanding of ourselves, for without it no relationship is possible. Only through right thinking can there be understanding."

As I listened to the talk, once more I melted away and there was only listening. And a tremendous feeling of "Yes, this is it!" came over me. I had found that which was of the utmost interest to me, that which was the core of my life's work.   I understood that this was to be my life; that this was my life that he was talking about.

He continued to explore the questions, to encourage the people to follow along in themselves, and, giving little hints along the way, he went to the depth of showing where clarity and order lie. He ended, saying:

"Through self-awareness and self-knowledge peace is found and in that serenity there is immortality."

Oh, how I wanted to touch that complete understanding and peace!

I felt extremely full and complete, so I slipped out immediately, got on my horse, and started away in order to be alone on the meadow hill above. As I rode out on the path, I felt Krishnaji's consciousness in back of me, looking at mine, and I knew that he knew how I was responding to the talk. I paused and looked back at him, and once again, in that awareness of each other, was that immediate acknowledgment, even stronger than before, that we had communicated on a deep level. This was absolutely clear, in a moment of direct perception.

I never understood why everybody that heard him did not understand his greatness. For me, there was never any need to seek outside of myself again, or listen to other philosophies.

I knew I was born only for this great work of understanding myself and life, and living in a oneness of being.

I had no idea what this would all involve, nor where it would take me. All I knew was that a passion had burst into my life, and that I was going to pursue it to the very end, if that were possible.

4

THE LIGHT
OF BLISS

Surely, we must all have had experiences
of those moments when the mind is absent,
and suddenly there is a flash of joy,
a flash of an idea, a Light, a great bliss.

OJAI 1949

THE LIGHT OF BLISS

Uncle José helped some of our family to escape
from Holland, although he remained behind to help
others. He was captured during the end of the war
and died of a heart attack.

His and my father's mother came to live with us.
She was very loving, and also played the piano
beautifully, encouraging me even more in music.
She always had time to teach me.

I loved her dearly, and we were very close. It was as
if I couldn't do enough for her to help her through
the difficult war years, and at the same time she
couldn't do enough for me to help me with music
and talk to me about growing up.

There was a deep bond of affection which I missed
very much, when, after the war, she returned to
Holland, disillusioned, and, having lost most of her
friends and relatives, soon died.

Living in Westwood was much harder now, as I
yearned to be in Ojai all the time. But we had a lot
of fun in the evenings. My father was still the actor,
and taught us little plays and skits, which my mother
accompanied on the piano. There was singing of
impromptu songs to put into the plays, and props

made to resemble costumes.

It was all very creative, and the emphasis was on each of us to create a character to join in the fun. We learned to be very good at it, and enjoyed ourselves a lot. This was before the days when you looked at television for your fun.

One day, having just returned from Ojai, a famous producer saw me in my riding clothes, and asked my parents to let me test for a film he was casting, called "National Velvet." They refused, knowing what kind of a life the Hollywood actresses lived, saying I was too young.

They only told me about it a few years later. By then, they thought I would not be tempted. I don't think I would have been, since I was still very shy and unsure about myself.

Elizabeth Taylor, who really wanted and got the part, was one year younger than I. She was also the daughter of an art dealer of a new small gallery in Beverly Hills.

There was a lot of talk about starting a Krishnamurti school in Ojai. I went around singing, "Don't fence me in," a popular song at the time, in order to keep reminding my parents how much I wanted to go there.

All the time, of course, they were helping to start the school, later helping to renovate the old Oak Grove camp buildings, and then building a new dormitory. In September of 1945, The Happy Valley School was started with great enthusiasm, and I was one of the first students.

We lived at Arya Vihara that first year. Rosalind had broken her leg, and Krishnaji, recovering from a serious illness, was staying at the main house until he was well enough to go back to his pine cottage. There were only five students, which grew to seven the first year, but quite a few more teachers.

On the first day, the key to the old cafeteria building of the Oak Grove campgrounds was found, the door was opened, and school started by cleaning up the building. During the first months, much time was spent planning and making divisions for rooms inside the large hall, doing plumbing and electrical repairs, watering old trees and planting lawns and gardens.

All this took most of our attention between classes, and students as well as teachers all joined in the work. It brought us all together in a closeness that nurtured a feeling that it was our school, and we were creating something together.

In the afternoons, when I practiced the piano, I was told that Krishnaji enjoyed listening to the music. This was the only time that I was not self-conscious playing in front of people.

Once, at our gallery home, Arthur Rubinstein heard me, but because I admired him, it really scared me because I didn't feel I had learned enough yet. However, he told my parents to continue to encourage me, to which they replied that it was not necessary, that I already loved music. After that, I always stopped playing the minute I heard people ring the doorbell.

When I studied with José Iturbi I could hardly bear it from shyness. It didn't last long because he was very aggressive, and taught the fingers to be like hammers on the keyboard. That just didn't feel like the right way to make beautiful sound - and it wasn't.

The life at Arya Vihara was fascinating. Radha and I shared a room in the upstairs apartment, there was a kitchen in between, and then Rosalind's room. Rosalind spent most mornings on her bed telephoning. Students and teachers were called in a lot to talk about things, so that she got feedback from us all. However, I didn't think that she listened very well, and seemed to hold on to her own ideas.

Every afternoon near sunset, Krishnaji would go for his walk, and most of the school went with him. We went up McAndrew Road to look out over the valley at the bridge, down Thacher Road, left on McNell, past the Monica Ros School - an old friend - up Grand Ave. and back to the house. It seemed everyone knew of this daily walk, and some people would even drive up, park their cars, and join us by coming in and leaving the group from different points of the square course.

In general, they would be very respectful of Krishnaji, and give way so that others had a chance to walk with him. He would greet people, but did not wish to talk about the teachings during those walks. He would ask what the news was, or about what they were doing.

The war in Europe had just ended, and people could travel again. Many came from all over the world to see Krishnaji. In the evenings, visitors gathered in the living room, and I always sat in to listen to the fascinating conversation going on. These evenings were an education in themselves.

Many of the visitors were famous people, and so they brought many facets of life into that room. Some of them would spend time at the school and talk to us about their life, sometimes teaching us some of the language, crafts or songs.

One of those early days, I explored the riding trails above the Thacher School, which was very near us. I went on and on, higher and higher into the mountains, and I kept thinking I would reach the top any moment and see the view. I had heard you could see the ocean, fifteen miles away, from there.

Finally, it started to get dark and, reluctantly, I returned. I was quite late for dinner, and Rosalind, who had been worried, scolded me about not being punctual. Krishnaji just listened as I apologized. As I was trying to get up enough courage to explain what had happened, he realized my embarrassment, and asked me if I had reached the top. When I said that I had not, he answered that I had actually been very near the top.

I was not surprised that he knew; it seemed like the most normal thing. He added that I only had to allow a little more time on my next ride, and I would be able to see the marvelous view.

This was the first time I felt a lot of tension from the Rajagopals towards Krishnaji, but certainly not the last. On the surface there was a lot of idealism in the school, but the actual facts of their differences slowly surfaced, and it was not too many years later before the school separated from him altogether.

That summer I spent much time reading the Krishnamurti books. I heard all the Talks in the Oak Grove, and attended all the discussions in our two homes. Many people came to the discussions, the various groups were of about thirty people, and I developed lifelong friendships.

The listening, learning and living the teachings was the most important part of my life. I realized that there was so much to be learned and lived, and I wanted to always stay with those things that had some intrinsic meaning for me.

I never seemed to have any interest in doing things just for fun or wasting time. I guess I was a serious little person, because a friend said that she had rarely seen me smile, yet inwardly, I was always smiling at the beautiful things I saw all around me.

I pondered over Krishnamurti saying that the Light of intelligence would lead to the truth. I thought that I really understood that. But I was making a philosophy from what he said about the thinker and the thought being the same, and that the observer and the observed were one. It sounded so right, but I did not actually experience that, and it remained an abstraction. It was quoted and discussed a lot in the groups.

Many people talked about how to solve problems -

but I didn't have any problems yet - and so much of the core of self-understanding remained hypothetical for me.

Part of that summer I spent with a girlfriend who had taught me about horses. We stayed with an English riding master in Summerland, just up the coast, where she learned how to jump her new horse.

We dreamed about going to India together. We both had a fascination with India, and were mysteriously drawn to it. The poetry of Rabindranath Tagore so inspired us that we wanted to go to his school. We used to try to cook curries and put on a *Sari*.

As it turned out, we both did go to India, but life had a very different story for us. While staying with us in Los Angeles, she met a young film student who had been interested in me, but I was not in him. They fell in love, and went to his home in Calcutta.

When her husband died of a heart attack just after directing his first film, only a year after they were married, his family threw her out. She was seen on the streets asking for assistance, but then disappeared and was never heard of again.

I don't know why she never tried to reach our family, because we would have helped her. I felt so powerless when I heard the news, and asked mutual friends to locate her, but all to no avail. For years, I thought that someday she would write or show up, and kept asking for news of her. I still wonder if perhaps she might be alive somewhere.

Once again, as with not becoming an actress, life had a completely different scenario for me.

The second year of the Happy Valley School, the students lived on the campus. Two of the old bath houses had been divided into four apartments, and students with house-parents lived there. Arnold Schoenberg's daughter, Nuria, joined and we became very good friends. She was a girl so much like myself - we loved many similar things. We spent a lot of time together the next few years, since her home in Brentwood was near ours.

Krishnaji joined in most of the school's activities, and was there for many school functions. He went with us to the opening nights of the High Valley Theatre productions, where famous actors from Hollywood often came who would greet him. He also went to movies with us in Ojai. I remember he especially liked, "The Song of the South." Records of "Zip-a-Dee-Doo-Dah" and other current musicals were played often at Arya Vihara.

The school had excellent teachers, a great emphasis on philosophy, and small classes giving individual attention to the students. There were two additional features of the school which were outstanding.

One was the wonderful folk dancing that was featured there, including the making of our own costumes for performances at school and at the annual Ojai Folk Dance Festival. I really enjoyed folk dancing, the music and the fun of it, and continued dancing whenever I was in Ojai.

The other was the high quality of drama taught by one of the performers of the High Valley Theatre, a group of very fine actors who had joined together. They put on marvelous plays of Shakespeare and Chekhov.

Our learning in drama was started with walking in a stage area and being aware of all the others around us, without looking in back of us to see who was where. This developed not only a stage presence, but taught us to be constantly aware of everything around us, wherever we were.

Once this protected me when I was alone in a city, and there was a dangerous man waking behind me.

I felt the intent clearly, so that I quickly went inside a store to avoid it.

Readings of Shakespeare's Sonnets and scenes from his plays were carefully prepared and performed at the school during the year.

We did not have a stage, so one day we all went out in a truck and cut some giant bamboo. This was woven through some strands of wires and formed a backdrop and entrance passage on both sides. It made a really lovely setting. Unfortunately, the Fire Department forced its demise right after the performance at my graduation.

I loved everything about drama - that weaving together of reality and inspiration. But I was not interested in being an actress because I would not want to know all the negative feelings of people. I felt that I didn't want to take on, even temporarily, those insensitive qualities as they might ruin something in me.

The only aspect of those two school years that I remember unkindly is that of having been forced by Rosalind to show off my small talent of singing - a Mozart aria of all things.

I did have a nice voice, but a music teacher from another school pushed us all too hard. Although he had told me many times to be sure to repeat a certain part, at the performance he forgot, and went right on. I paused trying to figure out where to go next, but he continued, making it appear it was all my fault, and then somehow ended it abruptly. Needless to say, it was a little disaster.

Krishnaji spoke that graduation day about the importance of living fully in a good and right manner.

I have very fond memories of all the kind people who worked so hard to make a good school. There was great affection, caring and guidance by many.

Dr. Guido Ferrando, the director of the school, and his wife, had tea and open house every afternoon in their home in Pierpont Cottages. We went there often to listen to him talk with people.

He also talked with each one of us, and helped us to clarify how we looked at life. He helped us search out what we really wanted to do in life, to find our profession, follow our interests, and encouraged us to live a full, worthwhile life.

The atmosphere of the school was very open, free, and nourishing, especially the second year for me, as I could walk from my dormitory up the hill to our house, and spend quiet times there playing the piano.

One day, in those lovely gardens of our home, I sat down quietly before walking back down to school. It was very still. I felt especially open and in tune with everything around me. There was nothing on my mind, and suddenly, unexpectedly, time stood still. There was only incredible beauty wherever I looked, and a special quality of Light pervaded me.

My inner senses opened, and I saw everything in a way that I had only seen in my sleep-valley. I heard the birds as if they were a part of me, singing. I felt so expansive; at one with all the life on earth and the universe. A great joy pervaded me in this moment of exquisite beauty - which remained with me as a fragrance on breezes of memory - and my spirit began to flower.

I began to write my first poetry when I was thirteen, and it flourished during those years.

There are some of these in the Appendix.

That summer, 1948, of my eighteenth year was filled with the Krishnamurti Talks and discussions. And, also, I lived at Arya Vihara because I worked for Raja in the Krishnamurti Writings Inc. office. It was my first training in general office work, exact proof reading, checking new published books and shipping. Raja was a meticulous man, and this was very useful to me later in my own business.

I tried very hard that summer to understand what Krishnaji meant when he spoke of the Light of reality. What was to be my reality in the world? On the one hand, I was very naive; on the other, I reached for an idealistic world.

There had been a lot of talk about starting a community of people interested in the teachings, as an experiment of living in a new way, without conflict. This appealed to me enormously, and I had formed many an idealistic image of a perfect society. I would live a truly religious life, and I thought that I would never get married and thus avoid all the problems that people seemed to have.

Already Felix and Elena Green had made adobe blocks from the soil of the Happy Valley property in the upper Ojai, and were building a house there. Annie Besant had bought this beautiful land for Krishnaji, and thought of it as a community and university.

I felt I had to talk it over with Krishnaji. So I had my first interview with him. I told him that I wanted to help him in his work, and was seriously interested in living a different kind of life, as he had been talking about. I asked him what my role might be; what I needed to do or learn in order to be a part of this community.

Krishnaji, too, seemed very interested in having this come about, and we discussed the importance of it. He seemed very agreeable that I could be a part of it, and told me to go and talk to some of the people who were making plans for this, and then to talk to Raja.

Everyone I talked to was very excited about it - until I asked Raja what I could do to help get it started. He only talked about the problems, the money it would take, and didn't seem to be very interested in doing it. The whole plan came to nothing by the end of the summer, as he did not support it in any way. The people involved had become very disillusioned and all gave up.

My first dream for a life that would be shared by other people, interested in what was to me an enormously worthwhile endeavor of immense value, was shattered. I thought that if people really wanted to do this, nothing should have stopped them, that a way would open - but this did not happen. The summer ended on a note of disillusionment with those people - not the project.

I sold my horse and bought my first car, and as my parents did not want to send me so far away to India, I went to U.C.L.A. My major was philosophy, but I found it very repetitive of what I had been taught at Ojai. More than that, I was not really interested in other philosophical teachings anymore.

Actually, what really sparked me was spending most of my time at the piano, and when a marvelous teacher who had just come from Holland came to meet us, I decided to concentrate on music.

She was Frieda Belinfante, a Dutch conductor who played the 'cello and viola da gamba. As it would have drawn too much attention during the war for a woman to continue playing the 'cello, she concentrated on the piano. She had been one of the five top underground leaders in Holland, and had barely escaped by walking out to Switzerland.

She was an extraordinary, affectionate, great teacher. Soon she was teaching at U.C.L.A. and later formed her own orchestra in Orange County, giving performances for many years. She also continued to teach.

I studied harmony, counterpoint and composition with her, and all I needed to know to earn a degree in music. But I learned much more from her about the meaning, depth, language and art of music. I immersed myself in music, and felt I had found the way I wanted to live. I loved it so much, and I truly thought I could find my life most easily through music.

But life had many startling, unexpected roads for me to walk on. And each one had a way of demanding my attention, at what seemed to me, at the time, to be the most unlikely moments! That mystical part of me still had a long way to go, and it, too, had an agenda of its own.

5

FROM DARKNESS
TO LIGHT

When you see something very clearly,
the seeing, the examination, creates the Light,
and the Light acts -
not 'you decide' or 'you don't decide'.
When you see something very clearly,
there is action which is entirely different from
the action which has been put together by thought.

INDIA 1966

FROM DARKNESS TO LIGHT

At that time there was a great movement in Los Angeles to allow people from India to become citizens of the United States. To promote this, there were cultural programs showing the arts of India.

My father and two prominent Indian families put on many of these events. He organized talent and directed some of the performances, and he taught me how to recite poetry to an audience.

Now my love for Rabindranath Tagore's poetry found an outlet. While I recited, the Indian students and artists played musical instruments, sang and danced. The ladies showed me how to wear an Indian *Sari*, and how they cooked Indian food.

Even though I met students from all parts of the world, the fact remained that I felt a very strong pull towards India, as if by a magnetic force. The Indian students from all three universities in Los Angeles knew each other, and there were many gatherings. They told me about the belief in reincarnation and karma. I wondered if that could perhaps explain the reason for my strong feeling that there was something that had to be completed with India. All I know is that I experienced a yearning, a pull, the sense of a necessity to go to India - a strong current of a feeling of incompleteness.

I was writing poetry now inspired by Tagore.

I have included some in the Appendix.

There was an amusing incident, pointing out the ignorance in America about East Indian things. At one of these events, Prime Minister Nehru's daughter, Indira Gandhi, the future Prime Minister of India, gave an inspiring address. The Los Angeles Times reported it, and mentioned how lovely she looked in her *Sarong*. Someone admonished the newspaper for their ignorance, and in their retraction they wrote, "We are so Sari we were Sa-rong!"

In 1950, my mother took me to Paris on a purchasing trip for their gallery. It was very thrilling to see the wonderful museums and exciting to meet many of the modern French painters. I was receiving an education in what was involved in being an art dealer. I had no idea it would be so useful some day. We had a wonderful time together. She taught me so many things about life. We always understood each other easily, and got along marvelously well.

We met our surviving relatives there, and also in

England and Holland. We heard their stories, and saw much of the destruction from the war. Each one had a story of unbelievable pain, yet a survival strength to go on into a new life. I only fully realized then how lucky we had been to avoid the war. We were filled with many disturbing feelings about what had happened to our family and friends.

The Germans had taken over the Ommen Camp and turned it into a concentration camp during the war. The commander had lived in our hut. Krishnaji felt that the property could not be cleansed and did not want to return there. It went to the Dutch Government and became a vacation camp for the government railway workers and their families.

Soon after our return, in July, I went with my father to the Krishnamurti Seattle Talks. This was a perfectly joyous car trip. We stayed on the lake with the Tylers where Krishnaji stayed, then moved to a small resort on a little lake nearby.

There were many people there that we knew, so we spent all our time with friends, taking side trips, going on walks and eating meals together. Many of those contacts were people who have remained in my life in one way or another. I was feeling a great momentum and energy for life, and thought that I could not be any happier.

When we got back, I began to study my first piano concerto for a debut concert. However, life stepped in and brought me one of those unexpected roads which took me in an entirely different direction.

I fell in love with an Indian student who was a prince, Narendra Singh Rathor, but everybody in America called him Nicky. He was by far the most charming, handsome young man I had ever known, full of artistic inspiration – and life to him was a piece of cake. Of course I thought he was everything I wanted in a boy – this was still the era of boy loves girl, as promoted in Hollywood.

He was taking his degree at the University of Southern California in Film-making, and had written a script about India.

The major talent agency had two of the major studios interested in making the film, and wanted him to sign a contract. He was offered to write the screenplay, and the position of technical advisor. But Nicky insisted on being the director, thinking no one else could do it justice. This audacity was a highly irregular, unreasonable position and, therefore, it lost him his big chance in Hollywood.

Undaunted, he thought surely in India, being of high birth, he could raise the money and make the film himself. This, also, did not happen, and his career chances went out the window. Unfortunately, he never did get a job anywhere in the movie industry – or hardly anywhere else – due to his pride in wanting to start at the top.

As soon as he got his degree, we were married. We had a story-book wedding in my parents' home, and stayed close by a few days, at the Bel Air Hotel, in order to say goodbye to my family. We flew to New York, saw the romantic musical "South Pacific," and sailed on the ship "Queen Elizabeth," to England. On board the ship, we encountered our first experience with racial prejudice – although very well hidden in subtlety.

It was a long flight to India from London, with many stops for fuel in those days. When we arrived in Bombay, it was extremely hot and humid in the old tin terminal building. The airport officials gave us a terrible time as they wanted bribes – but Nicky said it was against his policy. We spent half a day going round and round with them, but finally they let us enter the country. The ride into Bombay was an experience that one could never forget!

There was a long welcoming ceremony before the new bride could be admitted into the house. And what a house it was! It was in one of the best suburbs, a lovely compound – and 250 to 300 animals all living in it!

A leopard was in the room Nicky expected us to have, and all types of wild animals were there – outside the house, on the ground floor, second floor and roof terrace. Every kind of exotic animal was underfoot, sitting, flying, crawling, leaping, playing.

It was life in a zoo - except the people were in "room cages" most of the time.

Nicky's oldest brother had a remarkable love for animals, and he could tame a wild creature from the jungles in no time. The Bombay Zoo would call upon him whenever there was trouble and they couldn't control an animal who was in pain or need of some kind. He would approach it, talking softly, and soon have it so quiet that he could go to it and do whatever was needed for it.

We were known as the animal house and people would drop animals over the wall every night for us to care for. We never knew what we would wake up to!

For my first birthday there I received a little panther cub, and its sibling was cared for by my eldest sister-in-law. They barely had their eyes open. We used to go out on the beaches with the babies on a leash to exercise them, and it always caused a commotion - some people were actually afraid of them.

India was a terrible shock for someone as sensitive to other people's feelings as I was, and it always remained so. There was so much suffering all around that I could not comprehend how a country could let this go on when some people were so very wealthy. I learned to love many things: the food, music, saris, sandals and bangles; the countryside and its people. From the roof terrace, we viewed the most marvelous, inspiring tropical sunsets, and the deepest evening skies full of stars.

But the rest of the circumstances of our marriage were highly unusual, and from the beginning it began to fall apart. Raja visited us, in order to report to my parents, and we went to see Krishnaji. But when I asked to attend the Talks, no one was interested in going with me. That was another great shock.

Briefly, the family story was this: Nicky's father had been the Prime Minister of Ratlam State. After many years of good and honest service, someone instigated an intrigue and spoke against him, and the Maharaja believed it. When the Maharaja questioned his Prime Minister about it, Nicky's father was so offended that his work and character were not trusted, that he resigned and left the state.

After some time, the Maharaja, realizing his mistake, began to miss his Prime Minister, and sent messengers to call him back, but received only repeated refusals. The Maharaja then went in person and pleaded with Nicky's father, who declared that he would never set foot on Ratlam soil again because if he did he would die. After further entreaties, he finally acquiesced, and the family traveled back.

The moment he stepped off the train his heart stopped. He fell, and died instantly. His wife, Nicky's mother, took to her bed, refused to eat, and died three weeks later, leaving five young children to fend for themselves.

Although Nicky and his older brother were slated to become statesmen, and they, too, were entreated to stay, that same pride prevailed. They all left the state, leaving all of their wealth behind. They had been used to the equivalent of $500.00 a day for pocket money, and so they had no idea of its value. Soon those that "advised" them had managed to take most of it, and from then on they had to face the world alone.

The five brothers and sisters did a great deal of

fighting among themselves, something that I had never encountered before, and that atmosphere was terribly disturbing to me. As a California girl who had driven her own car and had much freedom, Indian life was very constricted. There was absolutely nothing that I could do by myself, because it just wasn't done, and because it was not safe. Unless my husband was free, or the other ladies, or even in some instances, if the entire family would also want to do something, it just was not done.

A lot of time was spent on people pretending they wanted to go somewhere when they didn't, the making of excuses, and a lot of rivalry among the siblings, so that in the end I never knew what to believe. I never wanted to learn how to play those games – as it was an impossible puzzle – and I left it up to them to work out and decide on any plans. They had a terrible time doing that, and it caused a lot of arguing, so that many times one or the other would not speak to the family, staying in their rooms for days sometimes. Needless to say, they had all been extremely spoiled growing up in the palace.

There were some parties at the movie studios where I was shown off proudly as the American wife. This was a great coup in the Indian film society – although the second largest in the world – as American films and the life they depicted were looked up to and imitated a great deal in those days.

I started to wear Indian dress all the time, and wore my hair in traditional ways, so many people thought I was Indian. It's funny, no matter what country I have been to in the world, people always think I'm a native - until I open my mouth.

Life for me was as if I stood still on quicksand. So I spent a lot of time playing an old upright piano they had bought, while Nicky was out looking for a film deal. But, I soon realized no one liked to hear classical western music, and they could hardly wait for me to stop so they could put on Indian music. Another great shock. This one really stifled my daily life.

One day our oldest woman servant brought me a strange herbal drink. She said that I had lost a baby, which turned out to be true. She also told the family that I would get very ill soon, but they didn't tell me. I never found out how she knew all this; maybe she was just very intuitive.

But the fact was that a few days later, after having been caught in the first monsoon rains on the beach – a wonderful experience – I did become extremely ill with kidney disease and almost died.

My life was saved by a wonderful woman doctor who had studied in England. She decided not to do an emergency surgery, and instead treated me with ancient Indian Ayurvedic remedies. First, there was a long period of fasting, and then many natural remedies.

Then this doctor told me that I should be on a salt-free diet, and must not eat any eggs or cheese for at least a year. She said that I must start eating meat in order to build up my body again - that I had no choice in the matter, I simply had to eat meat. I had been raised a vegetarian, and had never eaten meat, fowl or fish.

At first I refused, but the family begged, in tears, for my own well-being, so there was really no way out of it. She started me on vials of chicken extract which wasn't too hard to take, after letting go of the idea that it was meat. But when they brought me shrimp, I just could not eat them. I had been told about little dead animals for so long that it was impossible for me. So I told them to disguise everything, mix it into other food, and not tell me what it was.

However, the consistency was so different, and, having to chew so much longer and still hardly being able to swallow the meat was a terribly hard thing for me to do. It was ironic that I came to India a vegetarian, and had to leave a flesh-eater.

But, I slowly recovered, and when I was strong enough we decided to go back to Los Angeles. When we arrived I weighed only eighty-five pounds. It had been a very close call. I was so disillusioned about India that I never wanted to go back again. I hoped that whatever my destiny with India was had been completed.

Nicky could not find work that suited him, although assistant director jobs were offered. Life became very hard.

I regained my health quite fast, and yearned for a child who would love music and be interested in the Krishnamurti teachings. Thus, I, too, without knowing at that time what my parents had done, attracted such a loving entity to me. My son, Rajendra, turned out to be all I ever dreamed of, and we are very close and alike in spirit. Although I also wanted a daughter, I never had another child.

The Indian family demanded that we come back to show our baby Raji to them. Nicky was drinking a lot of alcohol by then, and I saw that it was getting out of control. I knew he would not drink in India, out of respect for his older brother and the family, so I reluctantly agreed to go and try living there again.

When Raji was a year and a half, we took him to meet the family. It was no good, however; all the same old problems came up all over again, and many new ones were there for the family. Nothing worked out. The family relied on Nicky to save them from severe money problems.

Raji was ill everyday he was there, from the intolerable climate of Bombay.

After more than a year of this, and due to the financial problems, we decided to go back to the States. Nicky went ahead to get a place for us. We set a date, and although Raji was running a high fever with double dysentery, I insisted on going that date anyway as planned.

On the plane he recovered very fast. On the stop in France, he was running around feeling good. On a very stormy, bumpy ride into New York, he was the only one who did not get ill, but was actually helping others by running errands.

Things did not improve in our life, nor in our

relationship. I felt I was bound to remain in the marriage, as the idea of separation meant failure to me. I was completely attached to my husband, and to the image of what marriage was supposed to be. I wanted to try to make it work out, especially for the sake of our son.

Nicky was now drinking very heavily, and lost the only job he had ever had. He was totally dependent on me doing everything for him, for Raji, and for running the house.

In 1956, I thought that the only thing to do was to move to Ojai where my parents were now retired. We rented a house, and I got a job teaching in the Monica Ros School. This was an exceptional place, run by a lovely great lady from Australia who was a friend of Krishnaji's, and truly understood the teachings and what they meant in the education of children. So this enabled my little four-year-old son to go there. He flourished in the atmosphere. I had a class of ten, three-year-old darlings, and I loved the job.

Nicky tried starting a photography studio in our house, but it never came to anything because he asked exorbitant prices.

Soon he became very ill, disoriented, and a great change came over his personality. He would be very inspired, talking wildly about all the movies he was going to make, then become extremely depressed, withdrawn and feeling great self-pity for all the imagined wrongs in his life.

He would wake up at night, have hallucinations, and threaten not only me, but Raji, too, whom he awakened to yell at. Several times he attacked me and cut me with a knife. The next morning, he would remember nothing about it, and deny the whole thing. I tried to remain awake at night to protect myself and Raji – once succeeding in doing so for seven nights.

Finally, I confided in a friend, the mother of one of my students, who advised me to call her doctor for help. Dr. Ray Huckins was a great diagnostician, and a marvelous healer who was respected and loved by many people. He could have had his practice in any of the most important hospitals and research centers in the U.S., but chose to be a family practitioner.

He immediately suspected that Nicky had a certain very rare chemical imbalance disease. The tests proved negative, but he didn't trust them, since the illness was rarely seen outside of India. He spent seven days in his office lab devising a new test, which is now the standard one used. This disease manifests in a great build-up in the body of a certain harmful chemical, and the excess causes violence and temporary insanity. It was incurable.

Dr. Huckins told Nicky that drinking alcohol was extremely harmful and that he must quit it. Nicky, who didn't want anybody to know that he had any weakness, quit immediately. Dr. Huckins had told my friend to invite us over to her house for a game of cards, so he could be on hand to help as he knew what would happen.

Within a few hours Nicky was thrown into convulsions, as Dr. Huckins had expected, and he had to be rushed to the Cottage Hospital in Santa Barbara. Dr. Huckins stayed in the back seat administering to Nicky while I drove. What a remarkable, caring man he is. The prognosis among the doctors was that Nicky was not expected to live through this attack.

He remained out of his mind, not knowing where he was, for eighteen days. He accused me of his situation, and violently attacked me and all the caretakers, also, so he had to be strapped down. I was told it was better to not even try to see him as long as he was like this.

I remained in the hospital most of the time, staying in a motel nearby, while Raji was taken care of by this same dear lady who had helped me, and by my parents.

But, then, I was told he would recover for a short while, but was not expected to live for more than six months. He could go home in a few days, but nobody knew how long it would be before the next attack.

This threw me into a panic state! What was I to do? There seemed no answer. This was the one time I did not tell my parents, nor anyone else, what the extent of the problem was, and that the illness would recur again with violence. I really thought that I must live with the problem, and make the best of things.

For the moment, Nicky seemed all right. He had no memory of the events in the hospital, so he totally denied that he was ill, saying it was only withdrawal symptoms from stopping the drinking.

My mother found a little gift shop for sale in town, and said she would show me how to run a business, as my father offered to buy it for us. This gave us a chance to earn a living, and, for a while, Nicky was interested in it, too.

We put in Indian jewelry and crafts imported by our

family friends in Los Angeles; found unusual gifts; displayed Beatrice Wood pottery; the work of local artists; and also showed paintings and fine lithographs from my father's collection of modern French art. I really enjoyed turning the place into a fine art gallery - the first in Ojai. On a whim, I called it, "Galerie Gabriele."

Things went along pretty well for a while until the illness again built up and ruined any peace of mind. This time I was desperate, and spent all my time trying to figure out what to do about being at the business, taking care to protect my son, and going home to the violence.

I was in great darkness searching for Light. Krishnaji had said many times that when you come out of darkness, that darkness ends. I had no idea how I would resolve the darkness. I decided that there was only one person who could help me find out what to do, and that was Krishnaji. Luckily he was to have lunch at my parents' house the very next day after I decided to ask him for help and clarity.

So I telephoned Krishnaji, and I had an interview with him. This extraordinary interview completely changed my life.

When we met, I wanted to tell him so many things about our life, and how it had all gone wrong. I still loved Nicky but found the problems completely overwhelming. I wanted to explain how his now total dependence on me was an impossible situation, and to ask him how I could possibly let go of a dying man's hand. So I met him full of things to say and ask.

But, he would not let me tell him anything! I was completely set back when he said he knew the situation. I could not accept this at first, thinking that he thought it was the usual marital problem of incompatibility. So I kept on trying to explain. But he would have none of it - repeating that he knew everything!

It was as if the moment we met, he had instantly tuned into me, and somehow had awareness of the entire circumstances and situation. He placed his hand on my knee for a moment in a loving gesture, and suggested that we find out what was the best for the father, for the child, and for the mother. I stopped trying to tell him things, and my listening began.

He asked questions in order for us to focus on each of the three participants objectively, and thereby helped me to see the situation as it actually was. From these questions, I realized in amazement that he really did know all that was involved. I began to understand the situation.

Krishnaji helped me to see that the father needed a great deal of care which I couldn't provide, as I had the business, our son, and the house to take care of. I saw that the father had been so occupied with his own problems, that although he loved his son, he had really spent very little time with him.

Krishnaji showed me that the child would not miss the father too much as he was a little bit afraid of him, and that they had done very few things together. I also saw that the boy needed a gentle environment to nourish his very sensitive nature, and that I must provide that for him. Krishnaji even explained that since I had asked for this special child, it was my primary obligation to care for his welfare. He even knew about that!

And then, Krishnaji helped me see that I was not responsible for the very different temperament and cultural differences which caused problems between us, nor for the tragedies of Nicky's earlier life which caused the great pride which held him back from life.

He also said that I was not responsible for his illness, and that if my husband were to die, my concern must first be for the child. However, he carefully explained that whether he died or not was not up to me in any way, and that any action I took could not influence that event.

As I sat there, stunned, contemplating the truth of the matter, I wondered how in the world I would go about this without causing great hurt, and who would take care of Nicky. Krishnaji knew my thoughts, and proceeded to speak about this reality, in terms of the kindest way to go about the separation.

He suggested that perhaps I could send Nicky to India to see his family, and to purchase some supplies for the gallery. He explained that Nicky really belonged in India, as he felt more at home there, and his family would care for him because that was the tradition.

He suggested that I write a letter to him, and also to the family upon his arrival, explaining everything about the illness, and telling them how I felt about the marriage and why I could not go on with it anymore.

I realized that my energies must be for my child now, and promised to do my utmost in his upbringing.

After we had looked at the situation objectively, as it actually was, it had all suddenly become very clear.

Krishnaji shone the Light of clarity which brought understanding. The tremendous weight of the burden had shifted into new energy for what I felt had to be done.

I thanked Krishnaji profusely, but he only laughed, saying that I might have seen it for myself if I had not been so emotionally attached. Thus, he gave me the clue to the cause of my sorrow, which I knew I had to work through if I ever wanted to be free.

We walked out of the room together, and I immediately told my parents that I was going to divorce Nicky. They were so surprised, but Krishnaji also told them that I had to do it; that there was no other way. We both quickly told them the story and what needed to be done. They said they would help.

And so I did it all just as he had suggested. What happened was that when the letters arrived in India, no one believed me. Within two days, my future ex-husband flew back and rang my doorbell. He tried to change things by talking about them, and begged me to stay with him. I had never told him how I really felt because I was afraid of what that might provoke.

But after going over it with him, he did see that I just could not go on as before. He said he did not blame me in any way, and that he knew it was all his fault, and would accept my decision. I responded that it was a tragedy, perhaps no one was to blame, but that we must resolve it, and go on with our lives, being as clear as we could. I never heard anything from the family in India.

So that was the end of a ten-year relationship. It was also the first time I had ever said, "No, I can't do things your way." It was a terribly hard lesson, but it changed my life completely. I knew now that the obligation to India was finally completed.

Oh, but not my suffering! I had been so attached to the man and the whole conventional image of what marriage should be, that I had to do a great deal of work on myself in order to get free from that terrible suffering. I spent all my evenings and any free time reading the Krishnamurti books, finding out about looking at the problems and blocks in myself.

I had to observe the patterns and limitations I had boxed myself into. I had to learn how my images had been started and formed long ago. I had to see how I had not just fallen in love from one moment to the next, but that that action had very deep roots in everything I had thought, imagined, wished for and desired.

It took quite a while to free myself from the whole dark misery I was feeling. I had to clarify my thoughts and feelings, and let the Light of understanding bring freedom. I had to learn about the attachment and dependency, and look at my loneliness and confusion, before I could find a totally new way of living my life.

I wrote some very emotional, revealing poetry, and made a recording of it, reciting it to a Brahms piano concerto.

Perhaps others going through a similar experience might find some clarity in them, so I have included them in the Appendix.

So, somehow, I stumbled out of the pain, feeling raw and very vulnerable. But the darkness had ended, and there was Light in my life.

In that interview, Krishnaji had not spoken to me as an authority because we discussed the entire situation. He had taught me how to be a Light unto myself. I realized that being a Light unto oneself truly meant freedom from dependency and authority.

We heard nothing from my son's father for the next eleven years - no letter, no birthday card, no gift for his son - no contact at all. Friends thought he was in India. Then one summer while I was in Saanen, and Raji had remained in Ojai, a mutual friend contacted Raji and told him that his father would like to see him. They got to know each other, becoming friends. I was very happy that they had some time together.

He came to Ojai to live, and asked me to meet him once. But we never said anything about the past to each other – all the doors had been closed – and there was nothing to talk about. It was as if it had all occurred in another life. And, indeed, my life had changed so much that it was entirely different. I was surprised to learn that he had married, and had a little daughter. He was still drinking and using some drugs. He died a few years later.

6

THE LIGHT
THAT RESOLVES

When you are so alert, watching, observing,
it is like putting great Light
on the thing which you observe.
Then it disappears totally,
never to return.

MIND WITHOUT MEASURE 1983

THE LIGHT THAT RESOLVES

It was 1960, and now I was on my own, but still not completely free from the trauma from the experiences of the past ten years.

I was still shy, of course, but more than that, I was so enclosed in myself that I did not open up to life or people. I was very afraid of having another relationship, and the thought of another marriage was completely out of the question.

I invited friends over, and started a discussion group. This was of immense help to me after years of living a very isolated life. One of these friends, who had known our family a long time, fell in love with me, and suggested I go to see someone who had helped him and many other people with deep psychological problems. This friend, Albert Blackburn, was to become my second husband.

But first I had to break down the walls and barriers that I had built around myself. So I agreed to give it a try.

He took me to Los Angeles to meet Phyllis Krystal, a psychotherapist of the Jungian school, who was born in England. We talked a while, and then in one session of about an hour and a half, she helped me to completely release myself.

I was absolutely amazed. Her way of showing me how to go inside myself in a deep, relaxed, visual experiential meditation was phenomenal. This meditation session, like a waking dream state - but one in which I could act freely and make decisions and choices - revealed the problem through the symbols of my thoughts and feelings.

I realized all the subtler implications of the whole situation, and by working through them, they were completely resolved. That one work really freed me from the residue of that past involvement, and I was able to let go of those last negative attachments which had tied me to my husband, and to the idea and image of marriage.

I had found not only a new way to live, but a work which I deeply felt I wanted to learn in order to pass this type of healing on to others. When I asked Phyllis to teach me, she saw that I was serious, and suggested we inquire together whether it was really what I was ready to learn.

Together, we tuned into "The Light" which always guides our work. Through a deep inquiry into myself to see if there was any selfish motivation, and through a type of initiation, we found out that I was ready to learn.

This work is only properly done by someone who can let his or her conscious mind and any ideas about a problem stay out of the way. Then there is only questioning and gentle guidance for the patient who, of course, has to find his or her own answers.

This work is not on a conscious analytical level, and each patient - although having problems similar to many other people - finds his or her own way through it, and resolves it through the connection of the Light and his or her own innate wisdom.

Phyllis and I became friends, worked together, and explored many facets of this work. I learned everything - not only from her - but from the 'inside', being one with the Light, which represents the sources of the highest wisdom and truth. We continued to work very intensely together for the next few years, and we learned about the tremendous capacity of this work.

Quite remarkably, there is always a way to resolve the many types of problems people have. We were taught a way to get insights for other people to aid them in their own work on themselves. And also, we were taught what could be done when they could not do work themselves; how we could do healing work for them.

We were also led into areas of past lives, when there

had been trauma resulting in present inexplicable physical or emotional problems.

We were shown how those influences needed to be resolved before healing in the present was possible.

We were further shown how to help people who had died and were causing problems to their family because they were not released. And, we were also taught new areas of healing the body.

It was very clearly shown by the Light that I was not to concentrate on any one method of healing work. I was to explore and learn from many different healing capacities. This led me to many diverse and intense energies, all of which are there for me to use now when appropriate. I truly consider all of this work spiritual healing.

I have now been working with people for over thirty years, and find each session has something new to teach me as well as the patient. This meditative work is also very wonderful for people who are serious about freeing themselves, and "living in a different way," as Krishnamurti talked about so often.

Those two years of 1961 and 1962, for the first time

being on my own, were a time of tremendously hard work on myself. I truly applied all my studying of the teachings to myself, and began to slowly live an entirely different life. I had some deep insights which brought not only sanity, but expansion to my life. They led to some tremendous breakthroughs, and the Light of freedom, which showed glimpses of experiencing that state of a quiet mind.

In the spring of 1962 my parents and many friends were planning to go to the Saanen, Switzerland Talks. I longed to go also, but could not afford it. I allowed myself to get very upset about the situation, wishing for something I couldn't have - like a spoiled child. Finally, I had to give up the idea due to the facts of the situation, and I pushed it out of my mind. I consoled myself by hoping that perhaps I could save up and go the following year.

The next morning I arrived at my gallery early. I had just opened an exhibition of Marc Chagall, and received a phone call from a lady visiting Los Angeles from Texas. She asked how to get to Ojai by bus, as her husband could not bring her, stating that she had heard the pictures would be a good investment.

A few hours later she showed up, walked around, and pointing to one, she said, "That's cute, and so is that one, and that one." It seems an unlikely possibility for any sales. However, she decided on eleven of them, and wrote a very large check!

I couldn't quite believe it, so offered to take her back to her hotel with the pictures. I quietly asked the lady who rented one of the rooms in my building, and had the only bookstore in Ojai, to call her bank and verify her check. If there was any problem, she was to have me paged in the hotel. When we arrived, her husband met us, and everything seemed OK, although I phoned back to Ojai just to be sure.

On the way home, I realized that after paying for the pictures, I would have enough money to send Raj to camp and go to Saanen! Never before, and never again, did I have such a large sale. I don't know why, or if there is any explanation for it. The mind can make up a lot of reasons, such as, because I had let it go, it came to me. But I really don't know about all those supposed laws, that if you ask the universe you will receive - because I never asked - if anything, my state of mind was demanding! So I knew nothing about deserving things either.

All I know is that I had received a marvelous blessing, and I felt that I should do something to balance the scales, so to speak. The news of the danger of smoking cigarettes had just come out, and I decided that the least I could do was to give them up. I had been looking at the foolish habit of smoking, saw that it was not at all glamorous, and realized I had done it as a crutch to get me through difficult situations which I thought I could not handle. So I simply did not take any with me, and instead kept my mouth happy with peppermints for the next few days.

After three days, the craving stopped completely. It was not a hard thing to stop. Once you are very clear about a habit, it seems like nothing to just stop it. It is quite easy.

Al and I talked about the teachings, our lives, and everything that was going on with us and around us. We had an easy relationship.

He followed me to Europe, and couldn't wait to tell Krishnaji - they were old friends - about the breakthroughs I had experienced. He asked Krishnaji if he had some advice for me. I stood there more than a little embarrassed. But Krishnaji just looked at me very quietly for a moment, and said, "Keep moving, just keep moving." That's all he said. It was enough. I understood.

I kept that phrase with me all summer. It seemed hard at first; I had just done so much the last two years. But even though there was some understanding in my life, I knew I had to move much more.

I realized that it was necessary to be aware of my conditioning, and worked with that alertness, seeing how it affected everything I did. The Light of inquiry touched me that summer - and has stayed with me.

This was the inspiration for one of the songs I wrote later when I was playing some guitar and singing folk songs.

The following year was one of investigation for me into many new areas. I had found that I had some psychic ability, and Al and I had fun learning about it. I was interested in seeing if it had any importance in my life.

I learned psychometry, which is holding an object in your hands and finding out all about the history of it and the persons connected to it. Once I did a reading on a pot which led to a three-hour story, starting from the very beginning of when and where it was made, by whom and the people and circumstances of their lives. The story took me through all the people's lives who owned the pot as it was passed on to the present owner. This could have led to a book, but I didn't care to spend that much time on it.

However, some years later this capability led me into doing psychic investigations for the Stanford Research Institute.

In 1963 I sold my art gallery. I had come to the end of wanting to spend all my time on buying and selling things - no matter how beautiful they were. I had money enough for the next six months. Raj was boarding at the Ojai Valley School as I felt I had to seriously find out what I wanted to do with my life.

I was beginning to work with patients. However, I never accept money or donations as it does not seem right for me to mix money with healing.

This pause in the life which I had been occupied in led me to another great personal crisis. I found that I had a great deal of fear. Fear of what the future might hold. Fear of being alone. Fear of not being able to take care of my son, not being good enough, etc., etc., etc. I discovered that fear compounds into all kinds of rational and irrational fears, splintering off into absurd parts which somehow all relate to the whole complex.

I knew I had to face that fear. Krishnaji said that you have to go right through to the end of it. Oh, how in the world could you do that with fear - that was an impossible question! So I was terribly afraid of even trying that.

But the fears were still there. I knew that I did not want to go into any kind of future full of fear. No matter what I thought of, or how I tried, there was no way out of my fear except to escape from it. Of course, I did that - all the time. I was getting good at running away from it, covering it up, pretending it didn't exist. But when each day I started, I saw it was still there, like the monster in the closet.

So the day came when there was no way I could escape it. I understood completely how fear had blocked all my choices, decisions, emotions and feelings about what I had done, and what I was going to do with my life. There it was, and there was no escaping from the reality of the fact that it had stopped all my actions.

I came to the point that I just did not know anything anymore. This had taken a lot of time, because thought always thinks it knows what you should do, and is constantly busy trying to invent new ways to keep itself occupied. Thus, that which was the very nature of thought was now preventing me from acting. Even emotions and feelings worked with my thoughts, and together they had quite a few agendas for me to follow. None of them really made much sense, although I could have wasted a lot more time trying them out.

I had backed myself into a corner, and with my back against the wall I was left with the fact that I had to stop and face the power of the fear that gripped me. As soon as I was willing to do this, I had no choice but to let those fears overwhelm me, and be extremely aware of what they really were. In horror, I saw that it was actually fear of insecurity. I just didn't know what to do.

There was not a thing I could do about it. I realized suddenly that I felt there was nothing I would do about it. I just had to sit with those fears, and remain with it, watching it operating in myself.

Then it seemed like the totality of fear would consume me like fire. And fire it was, for it burned fiercely, and for one terrible moment I could not get away from it. In a way, it did consume - but I did not perish - which was absolutely astonishing at the time. It consumed itself! It simply burned itself out.

There was only a direct perception, and suddenly there was no fear. At that moment there was no 'me' left to feel the fear, no thought or even the name of the words, "fear" and "insecurity" simply did not exist any more. Any thought or feeling could not start it all over again. It had burned out, and it remained completely burned out. To this day the words "fear" and "insecurity" have absolutely no hold on me - they never come up in my mind.

The Light of awareness is stronger than any word, thought, or feeling. Intelligence will alert the body if it is in danger, but does not produce psychological fear.

This was the most emotional event I ever went through, but having done so, the Light of insight was born.

7

THE LIGHT
OF OBSERVATION

*To be quiet and observant is to have Light,
and without Light you cannot observe.*

INDIA 1966

THE LIGHT OF OBSERVATION

I was in love with Al by now, but he hesitated taking on raising another child. He was twenty years older than I, and had a married son, daughter-in-law and two little grandchildren. Although I still would have loved to have had a girl, I knew that it would not be appropriate or fair to him.

We talked about our relationship quite a bit, and just as I began to make plans to move to Los Angeles - close to Phyllis Krystal, so we could consult and work together - he did propose.

So, after being single for three years, I married Al. I was thirty-three, and it was like stepping into a whole new, different and exciting life. Al always left me free to explore and develop my own work – in fact, he encouraged it. The relationship flowered and grew until his death twenty-five years later.

Our deep interest in the teachings of Krishnamurti is what drew us together, and was the focus of our lives. We went to Switzerland almost every year, heard Krishnaji in the U.S., and were in touch with many friends worldwide.

Al had a love for the tropics. We spent our honeymoon in Hawaii. We went to Costa Rica and enjoyed it tremendously. We bought property, and spent a great deal of time there during the dry season. Al bought a plane, so we could fly back and forth, and we also drove there with a large trailer so we could stay on our property.

However much we enjoyed being there though, however much it seemed like paradise physically, we decided that we did not want to be there all the time. There were not many people interested in Krishnamurti, and not much interest in our work. We had a most unique beach property, with a tremendous power center, which finally became a National Park.

It took many years to work out a property settlement - but that is another long, long story. We did come out very well, though, as the government treated us very fairly. We invested the money, and were in a position to live comfortably without financial worry.

Al was recording all the Talks and Discussions in Saanen. Once, after the first day, he realized that the backup tape on the second tape recorder was only one hour in length, so he replaced it with a longer one. That tape was forgotten in a suitcase, and we only discovered it when we got home. The recordings were always sent back to Ojai immediately, so that there would be no chance of anyone hearing them.

We felt a little guilty having it - in those days no one had any - but listened to it one day, looking at the published booklet at the same time. We were absolutely horrified! The changes of words, the parts left out, the feeling of the continuity and development having been somehow lost - the whole life of the Talk seemed to be missing. Throughout the years, people had said that they clearly remembered the answers to their questions, and that they were not printed correctly.

We then took the few phonograph records available and compared them to the books, and again we were dismayed. Al felt that it was like taking a painting by a famous master and changing some of it because you thought it should be different. There seemed to be no end to the fussing with the text, as if the editor, Rajagopal, needed to show how he thought things should have been said.

We had heard over and over again from Raja that the editing was completely accurate, and that it was his sacred trust to do so.

We confronted Raja about it. He was absolutely furious in his righteous indignation, and defended his work. Screaming that we had always been against him, he literally threw us out of his house.

We then decided that I would transcribe all the phonograph records, and made copies of their texts in the published books. We gave these to Krishnaji. They were sent to England, and later we were all happy and relieved when the publishing was done through the Krishnamurti Foundation Trust in England.

In 1968, in Saanen, it was publicly announced that Krishnamurti had disassociated from Krishnamurti Writings Inc. All those who worked for Rajagopal were left with a choice as to where their loyalties lay.

Krishnaji called Alan and Helen Hooker, Frank Noyes, and Al and myself to Chalet Tannegg - where he stayed during the Saanen Gatherings - to explain how he felt about things. There were three meetings, and after the first one, Al thought that they should be recorded for the archives. Krishnaji thought so, too, so Al asked him to restate some of the facts. Krishnaji told us about many things that had occurred, and why he found it impossible to continue to work with Rajagopal.

These tapes became a focus for much of what transpired later. We were deeply affected by what he told us, and wondered if anything could be done to mend the relationship. We all told Krishnaji that we would do whatever we could to help him in the situation. We decided that we would go as a group to Raja when we returned to Ojai.

Frank Noyes returned first and immediately went to see Raja, who then refused to see the Hookers and us. Only when Al said that we had promised Krishnaji, and wanted to see Raja as an old friend, did he agree to meet with Al and me. We found a very angry man who said that we did not know what had occurred, and that he could not discuss it with anyone because it was a personal problem between himself and Krishna - he was no longer calling him Krishnaji.

When we stated that people had given money and support to the work for years, and, therefore, as a non-profit organization, personal relationships had no bearing on the facts, it only brought out a rage in him. He vehemently kept repeating, "He is not That!" It explained to us why the Rajagopals always seemed to treat Krishnaji as a child, and ordered him about so.

We did all we could, but there was no communication possible. Al confronted Raja several times more, and although he softened up at one point and even cried, admitting that he was wrong, the next day he reverted again, and there was no stopping his destructiveness towards Krishnaji.

Raja had many ways to exert influence over otherwise intelligent people. My parents and all the other board members just kept repeating to us that we didn't know the whole story, and that they couldn't talk about it. That it was a personal matter between Krishnaji and Rajagopal.

The atmosphere in Ojai, and all over the world, was one of accusations and counter-attacks from people defending one or the other parties.

We wished that we could just take them both to a deserted beach and refuse to take them back unless they resolved their differences.

We were traveling with Krishnaji in California where he was speaking to students at universities, and many young people were hearing him for the first time. I was transcribing the tapes for the English Foundation for publication, and also helping with some of Krishnaji's secretarial work.

Al and I remained friends with Krishnaji and continued to help him in his work. Even though both of us had worked for Raja in the past, there was never any doubt in our minds where our loyalties lay. Krishnaji knew this, and asked Al to be a member of the board of directors of the new Krishnamurti Foundation of America, which he was just forming. And he also asked us to be "one of the family," to travel with him in order to help in all the work and communication with the other Foundations that were being established.

However, one day soon after this, he told us that he was taking us out of all that, due to the problem with KWINC, in order to protect our relationship with my family. He did not want to be responsible for causing problems between my parents and us.

It was a long, tragic struggle between Krishnaji and Rajagopal. I will not go further into it as it has all been documented and reported by the KFA. Someday, all of that will be of little consequence, as the personal history of people surrounding Krishnamurti is not at all as important as the teachings themselves.

Nevertheless, that day Krishnaji assured us that we could help the work in many other ways, which indeed we did do. We always remembered that day, when Al again assured Krishnaji of our feelings for him and the teachings. Krishnaji responded by putting his hand on Al's knee, saying, "I know, we will remain friends both here and beyond." We never questioned him about this mystical statement, but of course, we wondered about its deeper meaning.

In 1969, "Brockwood Park Education Centre" was started, and we sent my son Raj to Montague and Dorothy Simmons, who were about to open the old mansion, to help them prepare it for the school. In this way, he was the very first student, and he - like me at Happy Valley School - opened up, cleaned, painted and got things ready for the first year of school.

That summer we went to "Brockwood Park" to see it, and to pick up Raj for the Saanen Gatherings. There was much energy and enthusiasm there, and we helped for about two weeks, putting together new furniture which someone had donated from Denmark. Raj was by now a very good guitarist, playing remarkably well and composing. One of his first pieces was called, "Brockwood Park," and mirrored the constant changes he felt were going on there.

Krishnaji told us that Raj was not too happy there,

and said that he needed to be with us, and to concentrate on his music. So we planned to take him home with us.

When we got to Saanen, we found there was a problem causing a lot of tension between Krishnaji's secretary, the school, and quite a few other people, and much had to be straightened out. Krishnaji handled it immediately, and soon things had clarified, so that the school and the work of the four new Krishnamurti Foundations were ready to flourish.

That summer we encountered another marvelous facet of Krishnaji's very special perceptions. One day, Al and I were invited to lunch at Chalet Tannegg. Krishnaji was on the porch, reading a letter. After greeting us, he said, "I have just received the most terrible, shocking letter from your father, Gabie - but he did not write it!"

This letter was sent all over the world and caused great mischief. People wrote my father very unpleasant letters, and accused him of all kinds of things, and, as happens in divorces or when one loses one's fortune, many so-called "friends" dropped away.

It was not until years later that I found out the story from my mother. They both felt terribly sad about the split between their two dearest friends, and always continued to feel that the teachings were absolutely true. However, two things tied them strongly to Raja. One was that they felt he had been responsible for carrying out Krishnaji's warning which led to their move from Holland, safely away from the war, and which probably saved their lives.

The other was that Raja had tried many times to convince people that the man was not the teachings. Despite all of that, the split weighed heavily on their minds.

My father had major surgery, and the day after, under heavy medication in the hospital, he was trying to find a way to bring Krishnaji and Raja back together again. He did feel loyalty to Raja, and wanted to defend him from the things people were saying about him.

My mother showed the notes to Raja, as no one did the smallest thing without his consent. Raja "edited" it, and the next day my father, still very ill and groggy, trustingly signed a very long statement. So, when Krishnaji received it, holding the letter, he could sense the truth of who had actually written it.

As the whole situation got increasingly worse, and

the problems deepened, my father had a severe heart attack. The doctors said that he could not stand any more conflict in his life.

From then on, no one told him what was happening, and he had no knowledge of the lawsuits, or of anything that was going on between Raja and Krishnaji. However, the whole atmosphere of antagonism and blame towards all the people who had been involved with Raja was so unpleasant that it considerably shortened his life.

When he died in 1977, Krishnaji telephoned me to express how sorry he was for my sorrow. He also said, "James was the kindest man I knew; he was never against me."

Only a few years ago I was corresponding with Mary Lutyens concerning Al's relationship with Krishnaji, for an upcoming book she was writing. I also mentioned to her this letter that had my father's signature on it.

She wrote me back that Krishnaji had told her that my father had not written that letter, and she asked me to send her an account of what I knew about it, so that she could include this in her book.

That same summer of 1969, in Saanen, I was interested in observing what occurred during a Krishnamurti Talk. I listened in that deep state of meditative awareness I entered into in my healing work. In my expanded consciousness, I went up above the audience in order to see and listen from there. The talk was about meditation and a quiet mind. This is what I observed.

As Krishnaji began to talk, I saw that a circle of vibrant energy was formed by his words and feelings, starting from him and drawn all around the people. A very wide cone of gold Light funneled down on him, giving him tremendous energy.

Going up from the top of his head to the same level from which I was observing, near the top of the tent, another circle extended. This circle was a plane of sparkling silver grains of atoms, quantum particles of that Light actively pulsating with the very essence of energy, truth and beauty. It was like endless diamond stars - pure energy, tremendously alive.

Every now and then, when someone understood what he said, some energy from that person would pop up and touch this field of silver, and like electricity there would be a sizzling, like a little fireworks. Then a fine line would appear between this spark above them and Krishnaji. It was a joining with the One Light, and that person would then appear more free, as if something had dropped away from them. So it was as if Krishnaji, through his intensity, joined people to the Light of Truth, to that higher plane just above us.

Every now and then, someone's attention would pop up into this higher plane, and it would be like a little ping - a little ball of energy remaining there for a moment, hovering, then going back down. This caused a little stir of excitement in me each time because I realized that someone was truly understanding something in themselves.

At the end of the talk, Krishnaji was silent for a moment, and his attention-consciousness came up also. As he did, some other people who reached for it also came up. However, I was the only one who had been observing all that was going on.

Then Krishnaji's consciousness made a brief contact with mine. There was an incredible moment of seeing in awareness, and being in direct communication at the same level at the same time. But, very soon Krishnaji himself stopped it, and as he went back down, so did the others, also.

It appeared as if there was no ceiling on the tent. The sky was wide open, radiant, and I knew there were others above us who had been listening, too. They were on various levels - the higher the level, the more advanced - all the way to infinity and beyond, to the Source, that Oneness of everything.

From that Sacredness came The Light which was so bright that I couldn't look up to see who was listening - and, of course, it was not necessary for me to know. I had found out that I could listen completely to the Talk in this state of silent meditation.

As we left the tent, Krishnaji turned and looked directly at me. Again, there was that incredible communication and direct perception. There were sparks in his eyes, as from the sparks I had seen above him. We smiled at each other, and it was a marvelous, completely open smile. Then, it was as if he winked at me - as if we had a secret. Neither one of us ever mentioned it. There was no need to.

When the first films of Krishnamurti were being produced, Al and I thought it would be wonderful to show them to people. We bought them all, as well as the equipment needed to show them. Our next project was showing them all over California. This was a way of getting the teachings directly to people who had never been able to see him, or who lived too far away to come to the Talks.

It is one thing to read books, and another to hear his voice on tape, but to see his tremendous intensity and expression when he talks is quite another. It was not financially successful, as we had been asked not to accept money or donations for the KFA - only names and addresses for the new mailing list.

But the project proved to be highly successful in that it reached so many people, and made a great impact on their lives.

We found an eagerness for the Krishnamurti teachings, especially among some of the "Hippies" who had dropped out of society. They had heard the gurus, but still felt their lives were not satisfactory.

Suddenly the sanity of Krishnamurti rang out loud and clear to them, and many began to read the books, listen to the new tapes, come to the Talks - and some went all the way to Europe and Saanen to hear him. We kept in touch with quite a few young people who said their lives had been greatly changed. They went back to schools, got degrees, jobs, married, and began to raise their children - pondering about right education.

This was the time that so many metaphysical bookstores sprang up, and since the Krishnamurti books were now readily available in bookstores, the teachings spread at an ever-increasing rate.

We were very thrilled about showing these films directly to so many people. The enthusiasm and discussions that occurred, everywhere we went, started a whole new era for people who were seriously questioning themselves and were so eager to do something in their lives that had great meaning.

⁂

Soon the work for Krishnamurti had been firmly established in the four foundations, and many people were taking part in it. We were free to devote our energy to our own work. Al began to have discussions in our home, teach some seminars, and started to write.

One day Al showed a manuscript to Krishnaji, who immediately said, "You know I don't read these sort of things." But he said he would show it to some people, and give it back the next day.

When we met him next, it seemed he would have nothing to say. But as he began to hand it back to Al, he just flipped through it. Suddenly he said, "There is some material here," and he stopped on a page, "that you don't know anything about. Why did you include that?"

Al answered that he had heard about it and it sounded interesting. "No," Krishnaji said, "don't ever write about anything you yourself have not experienced, as that is only second hand. Keep on writing what you know, have learned, found out by yourself, but don't quote anyone, including me."

That acute awareness of Krishnaji, like an intense psychometry, had gone directly to something which he then knew needed to be told to Al. He had not read it, had not spent any time on it, but he picked up on something that was needed in the situation, and immediately dealt with it. Needless to say, Al never did write about anything abstract again. But he felt encouraged to continue to write.

So, when Al finished his first book, *Now Consciousness*, he again handed it to Krishnaji, asking him to point out if there was anything that didn't ring true, or should not be said. This time Krishnaji held the book a moment, and then handed it right back, saying only, "It is all right."

When this book was about to be published, there was an emergency with the publishers, and they said there would be a delay. It had already been announced, and orders had come in for it. Another publisher was interested, but wanted to start the editing process all over again. Al told him, "No, it is ready to go, and I'll not commercialize it."

So after sleeping on it one night, we decided to start our own publishing firm. Al called it Idylwild Books. This was an enormous challenge, but we managed it quite well. I still enjoy running this business today.

8

THE LIGHT
OF THE WORLD

What is the cause of sorrow? Where there is a cause, there is an end. If I have cancer, the cause, the pain, then perhaps the cause can be removed. So, where there is a cause for anything, there is an end to that. The causation is a movement; it is not a fixed point. To find that extraordinary perfume that is really the Light of the world, one must understand the nature of suffering, the structure of suffering.

MIND WITHOUT MEASURE 1983

THE LIGHT OF THE WORLD

I was deeply interested in learning about the mystery of healing. Whenever you are seriously interested in something, and go towards that, there seems to be a law that it is also possible for that to come towards you.

A special healing gift was actually bestowed on my hands, but at the time I did not feel that I would ever be using it. Little did I know that I would be learning the art of laying on of hands from a master, but that only occurred some years later.

The first healer that taught me guided me into a work that I could do without a patient knowing exactly what I did. When someone mentioned they needed physical healing, and asked me if I could do anything, I would simply say that I would send some healing to them.

It was a long time before I became confident enough to tell people about this capacity, and then, when they were present, it worked even better. I was taught an ancient form of Psychic healing from a great Brazilian healer. I had to be introduced, tested, and was approved only when it was clear that I could work completely objectively, without any selfish motives whatsoever. Only then was I able to contact an area which the Brazilian healers call, "The Astral Hospital."

In this area there are healers available who have been physicians on this earth. They might be from any era or method of healing, whether medical, herbal, folk medicine, acupuncture, surgical, spiritual, or the laying on of hands.

These 'physicians' study and work together in that Astral Hospital, and can be contacted to look at a patient, and find out the causes of imbalance in their body.

Then there is actual healing work done on the body. Often they transmit healing through ways not yet 'discovered' in this physical world, such as the use of colors, sound, or laser beam surgery, which I saw them use thirty years ago. Whether through some ancient techniques, or through these somewhat mysterious methods - many times a combination of several techniques - healing does occur, and balance, health is restored.

They communicate what the patient needs to know, and answer questions as to what the patient could do to help himself in order to maintain health. They are always eager to communicate to me the importance of the patient doing the healing visualization they indicate, in order to continue to bring the treatments down into the physical realm.

In this way, the healing cycle is brought into the hands of the patient, and it is his own responsibility to follow through. Whenever it might be indicated, they will also point out the psychological implications of the physical illness, sometimes showing the cause.

Then when I work directly with a patient in an experiential meditation session, it is possible to work out the situations of the mental and emotional aspects of the illness, and release them. I have found these sessions with a patient to be the most remarkable form of self healing. When order can be brought to the mind and spirit so that it is in balance with the body, the whole person is in a healthful condition.

The interaction between the four aspects of man - physical, emotional, mental and spiritual - are very finely tuned. Each of these aspects influences the others, and as energy flows through one's being, they intermingle and affect the entire person's actions. This interaction continues until there is something that changes in the person.

The effects of this total integration – whether in the best of health, or in the worst of violent actions – effect not only that person, but all who come in contact with those vibrations. We do not, could not, ever live completely alone in this universe. Everything we do has an effect, and so every action matters.

I do not believe that all of our illnesses are always caused by ourselves. After all, animals get ill also, and have no psychological baggage that they are carrying around. There is such pollution in our environment now that it seems that one can get ill from the air, water, or the earth our food is grown in – as well as from the animals which people insist on eating.

When the time comes for us to exit out of the body we have been living in, it is appropriate to be ready for the transition, which means, that we must know how to die to our days and nights.

Letting go of the past, and living in the present now-moment is tremendously healing. It is so important to learn not to endlessly carry over our attachments and problems into our tomorrows. We do this constantly by repeating the same mistakes, patterns, attitudes, and negative emotions over and over again, which only brings disorder to ourselves, and all those with whom we come in contact.

The way we act in relationships, and the way we live in harmony with life is the whole key to balance within ourselves, and the only possibility to be at one with the whole of life.

The second healing method I came across was the ancient use of the Pendulum, known as Radiesthesia. It is a way in which most people can discover physical facts, even if that knowledge is not in their personal consciousness. We are all connected to the stream of consciousness of humanity, that storehouse of the collective consciousness which holds the knowledge of all that man has thought, felt and experienced.

When it is appropriate to tune into that universal consciousness for information, the Pendulum can be the instrument that connects us. Through careful questioning, it is possible to find out a great deal about what is happening in the body. Then one can discover appropriate remedies and therapies, and how to apply them. In this way, the use of the Pendulum is an approach to the establishment and maintenance of our health.

Thereby you take responsibility for your own well being, which together with whatever else you are doing for yourself, or with what needs to be done by a professional, can provide a more holistic way of living.

Wanting to discover more about the Pendulum's use, I did a series of psychic investigations into its potential. This led to sharing the many new ways of using the Pendulum with friends, which then led to my teaching seminars about it. But then, being reminded that I was never to devote all my healing work to any one method, and having the new publishing business, I decided to write a book about it.

I wrote and published a book called *The Science and Art of the Pendulum*. At first this was just meant for former students, who said that they needed more information, and time to practice and learn all that I taught. There were very few books on the subject, and none which went into it in the same way or so deeply, that is, by teaching a practical approach to health.

As it turned out, the book became very popular, and is still selling well all over the world. I still make the Pendulums and all the Materials that go with the course myself.

Al and I traveled and taught our seminars in the U.S. and Canada. I also taught in Switzerland on the way to the Saanen Gatherings. I taught these Radiesthesia Seminars for eight years, until I published my book.

Life brought me my next learning in healing in a very acute, direct way. One morning, just as I woke up, I had a heart attack. I stayed with the pain very quietly for a while before getting up. The pain continued, especially every now and then very sharply and I could hardly breathe, but I could just bend over until I regained my breath, and then continue my day.

I worked on myself, trying to heal myself, but my energy remained very low. This went on for several days, but things didn't seem to clear up, the pain continued, and my energy was barely functional. I had been born with a heart murmur, and thought it was just acting up.

Just then Phyllis Krystal called to tell us about a Philippine Psychic Surgeon, Feliciano Omiles, who was seeing patients in Mexico, near the San Diego border. She told us that he had helped her and her husband tremendously. It sounded absolutely fantastic, so, of course, we wanted to go and see what he was doing.

Al had neurological pains, due to damage from medications that he had had to take, and which no one had been able to help him with. Of course I wondered if he might be able to help me with the heart pain, so we went to see him right away.

It was beyond anything we had yet encountered. Feliciano worked for about half an hour on both of us, and then asked us to come back the next day. He told us to get a lot of rest.

When we returned to the motel we were staying in, we both fell asleep for a couple of hours - which was an unusual thing for us to do during the day. We woke up very hungry, went out to eat, and the next thing we knew we were asleep!

The next day his assistant explained that the body was tuned for this as a preparation for the psychic surgery. We had not told anyone there what we had come for.

Feliciano was in a very serious mood, immediately going into a deep trance state, and we were told not to talk to him until he came out of it. He worked on Al first. I saw, for the first time, how his fingers actually worked inside the body.

Then he came over to me and said, "Heart, Madam?"
I replied, "I think so." His fingers touched my left
side, and suddenly I felt them move into my body,
between my ribs, and even more astonishing, inside
my heart!

There was tremendous heat and a powerful energy
like electricity. I realized that he was working inside
the body, and I could feel movement both from the
front and back of my body, as well as from the side
between ribs.

By the time I had these three thoughts, he pulled his
fingers out of my body, and someone wiped off a
little bit of blood. He threw something he had
brought out of my heart into the fireplace and it
burned up.

Immediately, his fingers were on my throat, and
entered directly into the thyroid gland, sending in
tremendous energy which felt like an intense
stimulation, and which spread immediately to other
glands in the body.

Very soon he was out again, and his hands worked
on energy centers in the body, sending powerful
energy to the heart and throat. Again we were
dismissed and asked to return one more time the
next day. As I got off the table, I immediately
realized there was no more pain in my heart! It

never returned.

When we returned to our motel, we examined our skin where he had made an "opening" and saw only a thin white line, but that disappeared within an hour. We slept a lot again that night.

The next day, he gave us both another treatment to balance the whole body. We both felt our energy had been restored. Indeed, Al was helped tremendously, and I felt completely well, full of vitality.

My heart has never given me any more trouble, and our Doctor Huckins could never find the heart murmur again. Later, Feliciano told me that he had repaired my heart valves and removed a blood clot - which he had seen the moment I came into the room!

Feliciano had been born to be a healer, and had been trained for many long years in many diverse ways. His clairvoyance was absolutely the most extraordinary I ever encountered. He could detect the smallest pinpoint of a block in the body, and he could see the energies as they functioned in the organs and systems, thereby knowing what needed to be done.

He had many unusual gifts of healing, along with a

great capacity to read the whole aura of a person. Once in a while he would say something to a patient which was exactly what they needed to hear.

Of course, I asked him to teach me, which he graciously agreed to, as he said that I needed to "fine tune" all my capacities. We became close friends. We introduced him to The San Andreas Health Council in Palo Alto - the first holistic healing center - where I was teaching. Also, we met with our friends at the Stanford Research Institute, who were very interested in him, but could do nothing at that time due to their lack of funding for such a project.

We arranged for people to come and see him for healing in our home many times, and traveled to other places with him. We took him to Costa Rica, where he bought a small farm to go to for relaxation. I worked with him, learning the art of transmitting healing energies - laying on of hands.

Feliciano asked me to take over his teaching classes, as he preferred to work on people. I truly enjoy teaching people how to develop their healing capacity.

The few true Psychic Surgeons of the Philippines are a marvel to healing. It is illegal in this country to remove tissues from a body without having a license to practice medicine, and there is tremendous resistance to any alternative healing. Feliciano never made any "openings" into the body while working in the U.S. However, he had such tremendous power, and so many different ways of healing, that he helped a great many people. I saw many a miracle occur in his healing room.

Even though I never wished to work in a complete trance state, and therefore never sought that specialized training, I am so grateful that this tremendous capacity has touched my life. We worked together for eight years until his death.

It was Feliciano who one day reminded me of that special healing gift I had received to my hands many years earlier. He said that he saw that capacity in my hands, and wondered why I wasn't using it.

I still teach a Healing Development seminar, traveling to places where I'm invited, and people wish to learn.

Once in Switzerland, Krishnaji was suffering a lot in his neck. Al told him that I knew basic Chiropractic moves, and he asked me to try. The muscles in his neck were very strong. He said it was from speaking in public for so many years. I mentioned that it was probably also from Yoga, and he agreed. The neck didn't need adjustment, so I just sent some energy into it through my hands. He relaxed and seemed to accept it readily. Later that day I wrote him a note about it, but there was no need to explain anything.

When we met soon after that, he said the neck felt better. He just connected with me once again in that powerful communication of understanding, this time by taking hold of my hands, looking at them for a moment, and then at me, nodding. I felt foolish about having written the note - but I finally learned that explanations were totally unnecessary with Krishnaji!

Healing remains a mystery in regard to why someone receives a complete healing, and another does not. There is, of course, much one can do oneself to prepare the body for healing, by treating it with respect, listening to its needs, and doing all that is good for its maintenance and nourishment.

Similarly, there is, of course, much one can do oneself to understand our negative emotions and thoughts which are the cause of blockages in our body. Whatever our blockages are creates imbalance in our entire well being. Releasing those blockages creates balance. And balance is health.

I am not a healer. There is no such thing as the "I" healing. It is just the opposite: the "I" must be absolutely out of it. That means that anything I may have seen, done, or remembered as happening before has absolutely no bearing on the present healing situation. Healing is always new; it is always different; it is always something that can only be observed in the present moment.

There is only one energy in the universe, but there are many manifestations of the healing energy. Going deeply into these possibilities, learning about them, and finding out how to be in tune with the Light of healing, is the only preparation one can do. Then, only when working for what is the highest good for the patient, is it possible to have healing energies flow through one.

9

THE LIGHT OF CLARITY

*The mind must be clear, without movement,
and in the Light of that clarity
the timeless is revealed.*

COMMENTARIES ON LIVING V.III 1960

THE LIGHT OF CLARITY

The years passed, and Al's and my relationship kept getting clearer. My son, Raj, grew up all I had hoped for - very sensitively living the teachings, and in music he is an excellent creative guitarist, composer and teacher.

Our lives were filled with travel, teaching, being with friends of similar interests, and caring for our home and gardens.

Our love for the tropics inspired us to create as tropical and lush a garden as possible. Since our home is above the frost line, rarely freezing, it was an immense challenge.

In 1960, Al had bought a completely bare lot, bulldozed out of a shale mountain, and at first he was disillusioned that nothing would grow there. When he brought Krishnaji up to see the view, he complained that he thought he had made a mistake in trying to garden here. Krishnaji told him not to worry, soon he would have a great garden, and even large trees.

Al went to work on it, and planted everything from no larger than gallon cans. Today, people are still stunned at the great height of our African Rubber, or

Fig trees as they are called, and the extent of many tropical beauties that surround the house.

I knew little about gardening, and it has been a challenge to keep up, and replant some things I tried that will never do well here. The garden takes a great deal of attention, which I give to it, because it is not hard to love something so beautiful.

Something I did that was a lot of fun, was to invent a new type of Perpetual Calendar, consisting of a series of cards which are interchangeable, and on which one can put one's own photographs or pictures. We market it through Idylwild Books.

Another thing we became involved with was our love for the Tibetan Lhasa Apso dogs. After owning a few, and learning about the breed, we made contact with a show kennel, and began to breed them. I kept some females, and our friends helped with our breeding to their champion males. They do all the showing, and many have become champions, which is of interest to me because it is the best way to preserve the breed as it is – so many breeders try to change dogs.

Lhasa Apsos are the most wonderful dogs, because they were kept in the monasteries as guard dogs and companions. They are astonishingly tuned into one's thoughts, intentions, and feelings, and will respond accordingly. I love being able to raise these beautiful little puppies, and always find good homes for my Parti Lhasa Apsos of Idylwild.

We were in many discussion groups with Krishnaji. And Al also had his own discussion groups in our home and when we traveled. They are called "dialogues" now. When the focus is on inquiring deeply through dialogue, exploring together, and listening both to others as well as to oneself, great clarification occurs.

Al loved talking to people about all these things, and out of that, and out of seeing his own life and his relationship with Krishnaji, he began to write. At first he wondered about it, since he didn't know if he had anything to say that Krishnaji wasn't saying much better.

But as he worked with the writing, he realized that he did have much to say, simply because he had experiences which all of us go through – which Krishnaji had not had to go through. He wrote very simply about his extraordinary experiences with Krishnaji, and his books have been of interest to many people worldwide.

In 1985 we had a feeling that this would be Krishnaji's last year in Europe, and indeed that was announced there that summer. But although we would have liked to go one more time, Al could not travel anymore. His health was deteriorating, and we knew that he had only about one more year to live.

That summer Ojai had a tremendous fire which burned for many days and many mountains were left bare and black. Because we were here, our house was saved, although the fire burned one third of our driveway, and came right up to the back porch doing damage to our beautiful trees and gardens. When it finally ended, the whole valley was left feeling bruised.

When Krishnaji came back the following January of 1986, we could feel how sad he was for the beautiful green mountains, and all the wildlife affected.

But his energy was ebbing, also, and the mood of the valley seemed to settle into a deep sadness when people found out that he was leaving us. The following month there were several days of thunder and lightning storms. As the end of that precious life came, many friends told us that they could not sleep that last stormy night.

Al and I went to bed, but the atmosphere in the valley and heavens was of such heaviness and unrest – as if the very atoms and particles were scrambled into a negative energy – that I could not stay in bed. I watched the storm, intensely feeling the chaos that seemed to permeate everything.

I tuned into Krishnaji and saw that he was about to leave his body. Not wanting to intrude into what was a private moment for him, understanding that he had to do it alone, in his own way, my consciousness left his room. I asked The Light if there was anything I might be shown, and was told that I could wait and observe from a distance.

Soon, a little way above Arya Vihara, that great spirit of Krishnamurti approached, free from the body now. He was looking at his beloved valley for the last time, saying goodbye to it. Again, it was a private moment, and I remained at a distance, just watching. However, I knew that he was aware of all those who held him in their hearts and minds, even though the time for any personal contact was over.

Then he looked up, and the sky became brilliant with The Light as he began to move above the mountains into it. A great eagerness was in him now, to be where he had been many times before. As he moved up, that Light approached him, surrounded him, and drew him further into itself, as if welcoming him back. He was once again filled with exhilaration.

It was as if all the light in the valley was pulled up as he left, leaving a darkness and a void, and a completely static energy condition. Then his aura became brilliantly full of that very Light itself, surrounding him into a brilliance beyond that of even his spiritual body.

I wondered if I would see anything further. The contrast between his state of pure joy in The Light, and the sense of great loss on the earth was literally the difference between night and day.

Suddenly, from infinity, what looked like two distant stars of tremendous Light came down towards him. As they approached, I saw that they were of the highest spiritual Gold Light which manifested into Light Beings. They were of that same intensity of Gold Light as Krishnamurti now appeared. And then there was this great welcoming from the consciousness of the Buddha and the consciousness of the Christ, as the three of them greeted and touched hands.

Instantly, the movement upwards accelerated as they were drawn back into that Gold Light of eternity. It was not a movement of anything they did, but it was completely natural, as if they were going back to where they belonged.

The intensity of the energy was that of creation itself. There was a tremendous feeling of great completeness, now that these three were together again, and Krishnamurti was once again as One with The Light.

The stagnant energy remained in the valley for three days. It was as if everything alive had come to a stop. Nothing seemed to move. I didn't hear any birds or see any wildlife, as if they were all asleep. There was only a great loss, evident in the heavy atmosphere of sadness that pervaded everything. That dormant condition only began to slowly resolve over the next seven days.

The Light of Krishnamurti had been recalled, and it was no longer on earth. It left a tremendous feeling of emptiness, a void which had not been present on this earth during his lifetime.

That Light of Krishnamurti will not return. I was instructed in the most emphatic manner by The Light that no one would see him again, nor would anyone be able to communicate with him in any way. If they think they do, it is only their own imagination. He is not in our realm anymore, and the man will not be seen again. He is gone, as he so often said he would be.

The Light of Krishnamurti, as we knew him, has left our realm, but remains with the Light of the Christ, and the Light of the Buddha, as they were known on earth. That consciousness forms a trinity. Their Gold Light is as one with the immensity of that "Otherness" of which Krishnamurti spoke.

The energy from the source of that force is the Light of Oneness, Wholeness, Creation and Life. It is that Light of Truth, Beauty, Compassion and Love.

The teachings will remain, of course, hopefully in a pure way, preserved through modern technology. But Krishnamurti has left that which is much more essential, and will be carried forward directly by people who live all that he showed humanity. It is that immensity which is in the essence of one's own understanding and living in a clear manner, and which is truly possible through living in the moments of the Light of intelligence.

Al did not tell anyone that he was dying, and indeed, spent his time very much as before. He edited my transcription of the audio tapes we had published, which are called, *Further Exploration Into Now Consciousness*. This was the basis for his second, and last book, which he called, *Worlds Beyond Thought*.

He also made a great point of being sure that all his relationships with people were absolutely clear. He talked to many people whom he had not seen for a while, which was his way of saying goodbye. Only our closest friends and relatives knew that his nervous system was breaking down, and that he had little time left.

He told me that he had come in with Halley's Comet, and always knew that he would go out with it, not reaching his seventy-eighth year.

When he was very weak, and the ending seemed very near, he suddenly began to be able to drink liquids and eat some soft foods again, so the intravenous feeding was discontinued. Friends were arriving for the 1987 Krishnamurti Gatherings, and many came to see him to say goodbye. He had three days of intensive, long dialogues with them, about the brain and the nature of consciousness.

As friends were leaving Ojai, he sat on our back porch, looking at the garden, holding our new puppy, and enjoying watching Raj's first baby lying on a blanket in the sun.

He remarked how beautiful the garden and the world was, and thought that beauty was the last attachment, and perhaps the most difficult to let go of. I questioned him if it was still an attachment, or just an appreciation and a wondering if he would be in beauty. He answered that he thought I was right, and we dialogued on it.

That night the body almost gave up and he slipped into a coma. We were still able to communicate for another week, and then say goodbye.

Therefore, when Al was released it was not a sorrowful event for me - actually it was very different from what usually happens. I watched his consciousness joyously shoot out of his body, not able to linger in that body or room anymore. It hovered above the house. I quietly walked outside, and my mother and Raj simultaneously did the same thing, each going out through different doors. We all knew he was lingering there.

Instead of my breaking down and crying, as some thought was the normal thing to do - but which I never did - I suddenly felt completely quiet and at peace, in a tremendously high awareness state, just as he was. This last goodbye from Al felt as if he had given me a blessing as he shared this state of a perceptive silent mind.

Al had one last look around, impressing on me to remember that this was direct perception, what living in the moment really meant, and then slowly left over his beloved mountains, into The Light. It was an absolutely incredible moment of being - there was neither thought nor pain - only the complete staying with what was actually happening - and our minds were in a state of peace.

A year and a half later, I nursed my mother in her home where she died. I was now completely on my own, free of the past connections. Again, my life changed and I found a different quality in living in a new way.

10

THE LIGHT
TO ONESELF

One has to be a Light to oneself;
this Light is the law.   There is no other law.
To be a Light to oneself is not to follow
the Light of another.

KRISHNAMURTI'S JOURNAL 1973

THE LIGHT TO ONESELF

Oh yes, to live alone and not be lonely or bored is an art in itself! At first I felt very vulnerable, unsure of being capable of taking care of things by myself, and not having someone close to talk things over with.

However, I soon found that when it came to the physical things, such as taking care of the home and garden, or buying a new car, there was always plenty of professional help available. Those things were a challenge, but not really difficult problems.

For instance, Al had left the things that came from his childhood home to his son and daughter-in-law. I could keep them all, enjoy them, and then they would transfer at my death.

However, I did not want to be responsible for those precious things, so I gave all of them to the family immediately, so that they could enjoy them right away.

This left me with some space to renew the house according to my own taste. Finding out what I really wanted – simple yet elegant things, and in which colors, as colors are of great importance to me – was a challenge which I enjoyed tremendously.

Over the next few years there were many repairs that

needed to be done to the house. I took care of these, and changed a lot of things in the process, to fit my needs.

I also built a screened-in porch and deck, and this has been a wonderful place to have people over for gatherings.

And so the physical things in life seem to get solved quite readily.

Some recent poems reflecting my life alone are in the Appendix.

There are great advantages to living alone. One goes at one's own rhythm, not having to fit in with a partner's needs or wishes. However, this does not have to mean that one becomes hard, self-centered, focused only on one's desire. On the contrary, I have found that I am much more pliable and go more gently when there is no strict schedule to keep.

But the important thing is to live at peace with oneself, in harmony with all life; to live with freedom from attachments to people and the physical things surrounding one. Then relationships take on an entirely different interaction.

To live differently, as Krishnaji so often pointed out, means to me that whatever you do must be good, and have some intrinsic value, not only for yourself, but because it affects others and life itself.

To me, teaching and healing work with patients does not involve any kind of difficulty. When puppies are ready to be born, you simply act and do what is needed. Family and grandchildren can be a challenge, which can only be met with love and affection.

Life is constantly bringing challenges, and if you respond clearly to those situations, it matters a great deal, as everything we do has a ripple effect which goes out way beyond our personal sphere.

Living in now consciousness also means to live in meditative awareness of each moment. There is really nothing else, for one never knows what life will present you with.

There are times that a crisis in life can only be met in that state of direct perception. I have found, over and over again, that if I meet a situation only with thought, the action resulting from that just creates further problems.

How clear things become when you really listen to the problem, listen to the pain that others bring to your doorstep, and don't worry about what to say or do. Listening in the moment is meditative awareness, and out of that one finds the only reasonable, sane response.

There is no step-by-step climbing up to something that never changes, which is only an ideal image of life. One needs to drop that whole image of a perfection which can never meet one's demands.

Once in one of my dialogue groups here, we were talking of death and dying. We decided to experiment living with death as if it would be there that day. No way around it, you were going to die each day you awoke, and you had to stay with what you thought, felt, did, knowing death as an immediate fact.

It is not a great surprise that most things people do lose their value rather quickly. With the immediacy of that fire of death, that fact that you are finished, death is at your side - life really does take on a whole different meaning!

Each day that week I gave myself a shorter and shorter day to the moment of death, until there was no time left at all.

At first my attention was on what was left that was important, whether there was anything in an unfinished relationship that needed to be said or done.

Next my awareness shifted to what living really is, when the body care is no longer necessary, and life in continuity has ended.

Near the end of the experiment, when the self was no longer of any importance at all, a different quality to life was suddenly there. I placed no value, nor did I rely, on my thoughts anymore, and I watched them slow down, and then discontinue - but there was no fear or insecurity at all.

What is left then, can only be described as a living in death. Everything is surprisingly alive and new, and there is such enormous energy movement. There is only living in The Light.

Life is then very different, indeed. Attention to everything that comes up is there. When things come to you that seem to be a problem, they may need to be pondered on, thought and felt through in order to find out all the facts involved. But then that also needs to be dropped.

When time can be of no help, when thought admits it really does not know, when direct perception does not allow the problem to go on, then, the very next instant, intelligence brings insight.

To be a Light to yourself is to live with the Light of

silence which brings comprehension, and casts no shadow.

To live in tune with The Light is to live in freedom with compassion and love.

You cannot see this Light unless you know
the timeless movement of meditation;
the ending of thought is this movement.
But love is not the way of thought or feeling.

KRISHNAMURTI'S NOTEBOOK 1961

APPENDIX - POEMS: EXPRESSIONS OF LOVE

Gabriele

CONTENTS

FIRST ATTEMPTS   179

Including The Happy Valley School Years
1943 - 1948

THOUGHTS OF DEVOTION   191

Inspired by Rabindranath Tagore
1948 - 1949

LISTENING TO MYSELF   199
1960 - 1961

THE STATE OF LOVE   225
1992

And in the Light of that silence all actions can take place, the daily living, from that silence. And if one were lucky enough to have gone that far, then in that silence there is quite a different movement, which is not of time, which is not of words, which is not measurable by thought, because it is always new; it is that immeasurable something that man has ever lastingly sought.

TALKS IN EUROPE 1968

FIRST ATTEMPTS

Including the Happy Valley School Years

1943 - 1948

WINTER

A carpet of fleece falls o'er us,
Snow - bitter cold snow
That fell without warning
In the silence of nature.

A thick blanket surrounds us.
Fog - damp gray fog
Which crept on suddenly
In the silence of nature.

A hard sheet covers the rivers,
Ice - bleak white ice
That formed so quickly
In the silence of nature.

1943

THE CLIMB

Everyday I try
And many times I fail
But someday I might fly
Right up to the top of the trail

In order to see
Just exactly which road
Is the proper to empty
My wearisome load

Many times I climb
And many times I fall
Then start up again
As I hear that great call

One day I might reach
That towering height
With the winds and clouds swirling
With all that bright light

In which knot has my mind
Thus been winking?
It is that which is called
"Right thinking"

1946

PICTURE OF A KITTEN

This morning I sat
Among the leaves in the grass
And there came to me softly
A small soft mass

I watched her approaching
On four tiny feet
Then she curled up and laid
In the sun's rays and heat

Innocent and childish
She laid in repose
When a fly came and sat
Right on top of her nose

T'was a whirl and a frenzy
She darted around
Then she realized that fly
Was n'er to be found

As she scampered away
After I had caressed
I thought surely that kitten
Has e'er been blessed

1946

COME

Come with me friend to search the way
From darkened sorrow into bright day

Come walk with me out of confusion
And try to find freedom from illusion

For there's a road that we could find
But look not ahead nor seek behind

So come my friend give me your hand
And search thyself to understand

1947

ARISE

Oh friend
Sit not reflecting
Thy dull memories -
Awake!

Ponder not
Of vague hopes
Desiring future -
Refrain!

Live now
Nor past nor future
But in the moment -
Be!

1947

THE LOST MUSICIAN

These hands
Wherein thy true
Expression flowed
Are stilled

They write no note
Nor touch the keys
From which such
Lustrous music flowed

They were thy truest friend
Working in perfect unison
With thy will to create
Thy spirit of harmony.

1947

AMBITION

She sat in a valley contented at rest
While beauty surrounded like birds in the nest

She saw a small slope and wishing to rise
Walked unto its summit the view to surmise

Once there a low hill attracted her sight
And soon this was mastered to her utmost delight.

Up to the mountains she climbed till quite high
Each step to repeat for she could not satisfy

Always she wished further achieving again
Till then any higher she could not attain

Only then did she see when weary and tired
How the soul is controlled by ambition desired.

1947

IF YOU WOULD SEARCH

*If you would long
As the turbulent water
Groping to find
The reluctant shore -*

*If you would cry
Like the whistling wind
Through the leaves
Of the great trees -*

*If you would search
Like the blossom in spring
For the coming bee
To release the waiting honey -*

Then you would find.

1947

SENTIMENT

Oh look at this which I just found,
Is it not nice?
It has no worth save that of its own
But it is thine
And I shall keep it

It has no life, it has not light,
Nor can it move save in that memory
Which I store of thee -
But it is thine
And I shall keep it

So to this bit of worthlessness
My every sentiment clings,
For it is a symbol
Of that which I cherish -
And it is thine
And I shall keep it.

1947

WHY

Why does a heart disquiet find
When beauteous calm can still
The mind?

Why does a tongue displeasure talk
When in the country we may walk?

Why does an ear so biased hear
When little animals play near?

Why does a voice so harshly shout
When softening rainbows dance about?

Why does a mind confusion see
When bubbling waters play carefree?

Why does a lover try to hide
This only true expression wide?

1948

THOUGHTS OF DEVOTION

Inspired by Rabindranath Tagore

1960 - 1961

As a bird my heart flies to thee
For a moment it stays motionless
Suspended in the air -
And then lands near thy hand

The dawn of my heart is awoken
And the sun of love arising
Radiates in humility upon thee

Like a silent star thou came
And brought eternal Light
Unto my sleeping being

Thy face reflects
The gentleness of the stars

How like the tranquil waters
My heart waits in patience for thee
Even though inevitable waves of anxiety
Seek to hasten the moment

The waves of fortune
Glide into my shore today
To play with the sands of time

❀

There - in the essence of thy being
Lies the ocean of my love

❀

I am but the foam
Which adores thy ripples

❀

The waves of my heart shall continue
Their eternal path towards thee

❀

Serene as the distant mountain
Majestic as the ancient pine
Constant as the soil of this earth

Art thou my Lord

❀

Thy face reflects the same tranquility
As that distant mountain range

As the continuing
Crying of the winds -
My longing for thee is patterned

Just as the clouds
Shape patterns in the skies
So form I my life on thee, my Lord

As pure as the blue in the heavens
As pure as the green in the grass
As pure as the colors of all nature
Is the rainbow of our love

My being is guided
By thy hallowed rainbow

In all which is beautiful
I find thy beauty

In all which is truthful
I find thy truth

In all which is pure
I find thy purity

For thou art intrinsically
The all

I adore

The song of thy heart
The dance of thy rhythm
The poetry of thy voice

The art of thy soul

Like a candle is the flicker
Of my yearning heart
But unlike its inconstant flame
My Light of love shall not die away

I see thy face reflected
In every drop of dew

The harmony of my spirit
Unites with thy rhythm

To form the melody
Of our sweet music

I sing now all my songs
For thee

In harmony with my love
For thee

How often when my mind
Is at rest
My thoughts dwell upon thee
My Lord

My heart awaits thee
In anticipation
Oh my Lord

Though I seek thee
I have not found thee

May my desire deepen
Until the time
We unite in love

When I perceive
Thy utter simplicity
Thy deep sincerity
Thy lasting serenity

Then I conceive
The perfect balance
Of thy being

Thy great voice has so often
Called out to my inner ear -
And my whole being responds
In a restless struggle
To answer thy allness

*Now, there is, I feel, the Light of silence with which
to approach all the problems - the Light of silence
brings into being precision, clarity, preciseness to
the actual movement of every thought. It is only in
that Light of silence there is comprehension.*

BOMBAY 1961

LISTENING TO MYSELF

1960 - 1962

I

I have not listened to the music
Within me for such a long time
That now like a thundering wave of
Enormously complex emotions
All the little notes of the storm
Are clamoring to be heard at once

I am so complex -
I am all things

How can I listen to all of myself
At once? - Yet I must -
For the part would not be the whole

For so long I have been
Isolated - dead -
Controller of my every thought

Lest it offend him

But I am free of having to
Always be what he wanted
And so -

Ending up as nothing
Unsure - changing - according to
His sick clinging choice

Yet I step with the utmost caution
Hardly daring to step one foot
In front of the other

I have always been too cautious
Always lived in fear -

What stupidity!

Never mind -
There is the new

Start each day
Each moment afresh -
Anew!

I try - but I am bound -
Bound by my old habits of
Fear caution and guilt

Why do I worry about
What others might think?

I've put all emphasis on
What others think -
None on what I think

Again - how stupid!
They are caught like I am

It is my life
I must go through it - alone

I need not impress others
I need not worry

It will all come

Why think about the past?

I think about it in order to
Justify my actions
But it is gone - finished -
I will close the door!

The future will be as I make it -
If I step into it with the old habits
Then I will repeat the old

Why try to make the future into anything?
Let it come!

By being alive, aware now
Let the now shape the future
Come what may
There is nothing to fear.

No matter how impossibly dreadful
The past - yet
I have the feeling of loss

Loss of a security - false though
It was - an ideal:
The marriage symbol!

I cling to ideals for comfort
No matter how fleeting the desire
Mistaking the mere sensation for action

True action comes of its own
Not through desire -
But by seeing what is the truth

I was caught in the false
Illusion of hope

Clinging to faith is false hope

Hope is false security

The awareness of truth
Brings its own action

The experience of true action is faith

II

Why does my mind always reach
For a focal point to cling to?

I desire always something -
Someone - some idea -
Some ideal - some pleasure

Desire is always for security
Always wanting to capture a
Fleeting sensation

To hold on to time

To increase pleasure

Desire always demands fulfillment
Urging all thought - all reason
All logic to abandonment

I constantly feed the flame of desire
Constantly crying for more and more

Thus I hope not to see
That I am a dark void
An empty bottomless sieve that
Can never be filled with the more

How I desire something - anything
So as not to be the nothing!

The ideal of being something
Causes thought to cling to ideas

And yet -
That something is nothing too

And so -
I am constantly thrown back into
The void -
Into the nothing

Which -
All at once -

For a fleeting moment -

When there is no turning away -

I accept in silence
As what is

What is
Is then the all

What is
Is then the truth

What is
Is no longer pain
Or pleasure
Or desire

What is
Is the oneness
Of my selfless self

With the all

With the truth

With the love

With the god

With-in me

III

Memory - the occupation of time

My thoughts cling to memory
Cling for pleasure - even for pain

For hope
To hold on to experience -
To recapture experience

But memory is dead
And cannot be lived again

Thinking about it
Or trying to feel a lost emotion again
Is never possible

Therefore a vain attempt
A waste of energy!

Through memory
I try to use the known
To shape the unknown

I try to form the future
Through desire into the known.

When I do not try
To use the past
To shape the future

There seems nothing in the now

Nothing now -
No residue
No hope
No desire

And now
A freedom
A moment suspended in time

Awareness of what is
Now

No fear
No hurry to rush toward anything

Now

A peace
A moment of beauty
A moment of truth
A moment of silence

IV

I listen to a cry within me
A cry of such despair
And aching emptiness!

Where does it come from
What is its meaning

Why suddenly because I
Listen to my thoughts - this?

I do not know -
I cry out - surprised at the
Sound from within me -

And do not know anything but tears

I try to put a name to it
There is none
No cause - no reason

I try to change it
Deny it - drown it -
It remains

There is nothing I can do
To escape it -

It burns within me
Demanding to be heard

I feel it so intensely
Yet cannot hear its meaning

I do not want to know it -
I want to escape - yet
It leaves me not alone.

It is me - I am despair -
The ache - the tears -
I am the hurt

The tears pull me down
Into the dark void -

I tremble and fall

For a last moment I reach up in despair

Then I become immersed
Completely consumed by the flames

I have to submit to
The moment of agony

I am the agony

Again I cry out!

And then - somehow - gradually
It exhausts itself
It is done - it is finished

And - as indefinable
As it came upon me -
It is gone

And now - slowly -
Time and thought and reason
Once more step into my consciousness

And once more
A new cycle is ready to begin

V

A tenderness
Is slowly rising
From my innermost being

A tenderness so unexpected and warm
That it completely overtakes me
And I am one with it

Oh joy -
At last a sensitivity
After so much hardness and logic

Why was I so guarded
Never letting in
A moment of softness?

Gentleness is not weakness

Why was I so afraid
To recognize my own feelings?

And -
As I let the tenderness
Grow within me
I feel more and more refreshed
More and more strong

I am surprised that
I have not allowed myself
To feel it for so long

I am ashamed that
I have been so hard and practical

Sensitivity to myself must be
In order to see others
And life clearly

I had built a wall of protection
Within myself
Not wanting to feel the sorrow
Of others -

I had my own!

And so I became hard
Uninterested in anything
But my own selfish struggle

And even as I see all this so clearly
I do not lose this extraordinary feeling

It is as a mirror to my own self

How very strange and frightening
That I can have so many
Opposing emotions in me

I am so very complex!

I am all opposites - even though
I would like to deny some

I have known moments of evil -
But what use to think on it now -

I will not let thought
Impose in me now

For now
Right now
There is the tenderness in me

And all else is silent

It has its own magic
And its own healing

Tenderness

The very soul of the wonder
Of life
Of beauty
Of love

VI

A moment of self surprise -
How innocent I am
How vulnerable I am

Freedom brings an innocence of action
The only true action

Sensitivity brings a vulnerability
Uncaring if the ego is hurt

To be open - alive
Is to feel so much more intensely
Gladness - and sorrow

Awareness invites equally
All emotions
But thinking about anything
Can never balance them

To be aware - sensitive -
Thinking must cease
Then true action springs
From what is

Simplicity of thought-emotion in action
Completely destroys worry

To be simple - now -
Is to be aware of myself
Free of all desire
To change what I see

To be simple is to accept
What I see -
What I am -
What is -

Simplicity now is understanding

Understanding now is truth

Truth now is joy

Joy now is freedom

VII

Desperately I want to change
What is
I do not want to accept
What I see
I want life to go my way -

To change it according to
My own desires
My own pleasure

I do not want to accept
What I see as the truth

I want to make the future
According to my dreams
And -
My dreams never come true

I feel I have a right to happiness
To have things according to my plans

I try to plan -
To shape the future -
I dream of a pattern -
An order - a perfection -
Denying the truth of what is

And so cheating myself -
Lying to myself that
What I desire can
Be the truth

But I cannot find the dream -
As it does not exist -
Yet I hope for it
As all else is confusion -
Misery - struggle

The very struggle to be
What I am not -
What I would want -
Brings the misery

But even as I realize
My useless struggle now -
For a moment I find
I cannot give it up -

I still want the dreams
I still want the illusion

And so I realize
I am not really willing
To see the struggle at all

Not willing to face the futile effort
That cannot give me the happiness I desire

For the struggle to change
Is sorrow -
The dream -
The hope of happiness

And so I want only escape
Into the moment of hope

Yet hope brings me
No lasting joy -
Only momentary pleasure -
Lost again and again
To the struggle

And only the struggle lasts
Only the struggle exists
As the truth

VIII

Oh moments of joy -
Oh moments of truth -
Oh moments of silence -

I have known this state -
The state of oneness with myself -
The state of utter peace

This is the only thing
That makes life bearable
That makes life worth living

And yet -

There is also the sorrow
The loneliness
The utter despair -

Not knowing where to turn
What to do to escape
The misery life brings

When despair is in me
I can do nothing -
I cannot reason
I cannot think
I can find no way out

For reason does not free me -
Thinking does not help me

My emotions seem to rule
My desires for escape -

And escape from grief is not possible
As it brings only further confusion.

If a relationship brings
Confusion - sorrow
There is always the thinker
Trying to change it

If I want gratification from relationship
I am always hurt

Yet it is extremely difficult
To live from moment to moment
In relationship
To be open - aware
And not desire -

For I need so much
And so desperately

And even though I find
Much within me to bring happiness
I cannot live within myself
Alone - isolated

Most relationships become muddled,
Confused - stumbling towards a dream
Which does not exist -
And therefore bringing only misery

It is very difficult to be clear -
For I am ruled by emotion
False thinking - and -
The pursuit of the dream

Reality - what is -
I do not want to see -
If it does not bring me
My desire of the dream

And so I deny what is
If it does not please me
And cause further misery in myself

It is not the relationship
Not the other person that hurts me
Even though it is easier to say
The other hurt me

No one can hurt me - for in truth
It is I that hurt myself!

Oh moments of joy -
Oh moments of truth -
Oh moments of silence

A motionless mind, a still mind, is not decayed, dead, corrupt as is the mind which has been made still by a drug, by breathing or by any system of self-hypnosis. It is a mind that is fully alive; every untrodden region of itself is Lighted up, and from that centre of Light it responds, - and it does not create a shadow.

Bombay 1958

THE STATE OF LOVE

1992

BEING

I sit and look at the glorious sunset
Thought remembers how we observed sunsets together
Feeling responds with yesterday's emotions
Thought-feeling take me back in word - sensation - time

But then . . .

Awareness that these are memories of past events
    Suddenly sends my consciousness out
        Over the canyon and hills - and
            I hover in space like a Hummingbird

My heart is full

Now there is silence in me
Now there is flowering - opening - spacelessness -
Oh the breathtaking beauty of color and light

Perception in this moment of the allness of life - and
This everything floods my nothingness - into

Being in beauty
Being in harmony
Being in wonder
Being in joy
Being in love

WONDER

I awaken in still soft darkness
To the last calls of the owls
Eyes not seeing space
Warm breezes touch me - and
In wonder I rise to see the soft glow of dawn
Far away - yet so near

All the magnificent trees and flowers are awakening
Their energies flowing up through them
To the very tips of leaves as if reaching out
To drink the air and vibrant color

Now I see space - but it holds no separation from me - and
I merge with the first rays of sun

The dark silhouettes of distant mountains against sky
Are now surrounded with colors and soft mists - and
I'm aware of the earth and all creatures awakening
To this sense of wonder

How swiftly sun's rising transforms color into light -
Not lingering as at sun's setting -
As life's urgency moves into day

Now the movements of animals start,
I see and hear the songs of many birds,
Rabbits, squirrels and chipmunks in stop-and-go-haste,
A shy ever-so-quiet fox, and a marvelous deer
All visit my gardens

In stillness this sense of wonder of life's beauty
Moves in me - and
Transforms into extraordinary urgency - and
Wonder awakens love

COUNTERPOINTS

Great music nourishes my very essence
As it touches my innermost being

When thought does not re-form memories
When imagination does not build images
When sensation does not become desire
Then judgment, opinion, like or dislike
Do not enter to interfere with hearing

I do not use music for anything - as
I do not use meditation to achieve some end -
Motives never see that the end is in the beginning

There are only relatively few notes and chords -
But infinite combinations and harmonies
To write melodies and symphonies - however
The most subtle harmonics ring the truest

I simply listen with inner quiet,
Completely open - completely vulnerable
In tune with the harmony of sound - and in such moments
Unconscious, involuntary shudders of energy
Vibrate through me in spontaneous oneness with life

Then listening-feeling expands and bursts out from me
In ever-widening circles - and
Returns as a tender wave of extraordinary newness

Thus music plays with me - delights me - and
Composes a state of love - and
Counterpoints into my life

RADIANCE

The patient comes full of pain - emotions -
Attitudes - opinions and questions

All of life's accumulated hurts - experiences -
Accidents - inborn and acquired dis-eases
Are reflecting in the body

All that was lived by thoughts - emotions -
Willful desires and dream-images
Are affecting all of the cells - functions and systems

Where to start? What can be done?

"I" do not know - "I" cannot heal

So I let go -
And very quietly tune into a manifestation
Of the source of universal energy -
That Light of healing potential

Then all my inner senses become alive
To the needs of the patient's body,
And as the Light moves through me
Projecting from my eyes and hands
They know exactly where to touch
And how to transmit that power

And so - the radiance of the Light communicates
With the innate intelligence of the body -
Thereby restoring balance - which is health

When actually in a state of heightened awareness
Then - as when listening to music -
Spontaneous shudders of life-energies vibrate through me
And those vibrations stream from my hands
Rushing into the vacuum of need -
Thereby replenishing the life-force

Remaining always in a state of questioning
Intuitions come to guide the healing
Of damage from the impacts of trauma

When completely open and receptive
Insights come to reveal problems causing blockages
Which the patient needs to understand and release

My energy is never depleted - I feel elated -
Not by ego achievement - which most artists feed on -
But by having observed the movement of life
And its tremendous capacity for regeneration

Each time I am again amazed by the immensity
Wholeness and sacredness of life
In the state of love

GOODNESS

The first rains come after months of dryness
And the thirsty earth and every living thing
Hasten to drink fully once more

As the storm passes everything is sparkling
With brilliant jewels of moisture
The earth and all living beings -
From smallest leaf to giant Condor -
Rejoice in their complete openness and oneness with nature

My heart too remains completely open
To this ecstasy of interchange between
All the elements nourishing each other
With lightning flashes and rainbows

The clouds remain long in earth's reflected light
And as the sun sets that exhilaration and joy
Bursts from earth back into sky as
One energy of astounding glory of color

And then . . . suddenly . . .
A violet glow is upon the earth
With such unique beauty creating that
Great sense of balance of life

But not until there is complete darkness
And the new moon appears in stillness
Is there an easing quietness gently flowering everywhere
Into a harmonious feeling of rest

Now there is a sense of abundant completion - and
A calmness penetrates deeply through earth and sky - and

Being in that state of goodness
Is being in that state of love

JOY

The puppies are playing and learning
With life's energies flowing through them
And intermingling with each other

They are completely vulnerable -
Although mother teaches so much which they attempt to imitate -
Yet on their own they learn directly through cause and effect

Their innocence is very real
Yet how quickly they learn -
From the seeds of their innate knowledge -
All that dogs already know and need
To function as nature intended

They communicate their feelings spontaneously
In so many clear ways -
Using their whole body and all the senses -
And understand each other immediately

They run to mother - they run to food and water -
They run to me and all who come to see them
Tails wagging the whole smiling body
Always so eager to participate in whatever is going on
So that running-seeing-acting
Is all one movement of being-responding

Observing them reflects my own movement of playfulness - and
In that simplicity I interplay with their exuberance - and

In that joy of life
Is that joy of love

GLOW

The sky's sunset glow is the same color as
The waning embers in my fireplace

It has been a very good Sunday - crisp and clear -
One spent talking over many things with friends at lunch
In communication only possible with like minds

Words were not all important
Images were seen and laughed at from mutual feelings
Of the absurdity and foolishness in life

Two of us went to see and hear
The wisdom of the teachings
And related that into our lives and relationships

Then listening to some original music
Sipping tea and watching the fire's glow
We continued talking on the theme of this day
Further deepening the glow of insights

Now alone - reflecting on the day
And the blessing of being able to live free and open
My heart mirrors this day's glow
Of fire and sky - songs and understandings - and

Realizing that because sorrow is gone
Throughout the day my heart has touched
That state of giving without expectations - and thus
Has touched that passionate glow of love

HOLINESS

All afternoon there has been the presence of
This intense emotional-feeling state
Neither sad nor elated - but at that point
Where tragic and comic meet

No names seem to fit it
Nor have recent events produced it
Tears are imminent but for no reason
Of either sorrow-loss or happiness-gain

Hearing music has enhanced it
By inviting feeling to reveal itself

Loneliness may be one part of it - yet
The clarity of being-alone the other part -
Both are present - nevertheless -
One does not replace the other

Passion for a completeness
Is the underlying fire which burns
For a wholeness of mind and body

Realizing that fervor must not be controlled
Has released the tension now - and
There is only watching the movement of passion

That total attention to passion
Is love - and

That love of living completely
Is the wholeness of life - and

That wholeness of a passionate life
Is the holiness of love

THE LIGHT OF KRISHNAMURTI

··· Gabriele Blackburn ···

Published by:
IDYLWILD BOOKS
P.O. Box 246, Ojai, CA 93024
(805) 646-2646
© IDYLWILD BOOKS 1996

Paperback 5⅜ x 8⅜
256 Pages
ISBN: 0-9613054-4-4

Price: $14.00

The Light of Krishnamurti relates the many-faceted mystical and spiritual occurrences of J. Krishnamurti as experienced by Gabriele Blackburn.

This is the story of the author's life in relationship to these events, their extraordinary meaning, and the profound effect they had on her. In a simple, direct, factual manner, she tells how his friendship, personal interviews, and the understanding of his teachings, helped her to resolve a life crisis, and discover an insightful way of living.

This book voices the quality of the clear Light of truth which casts no shadow. It is a personal testimony to the sacred life and teachings of Krishnamurti, that Gold Light of eternity.

Gabriele Blackburn is a spiritual healer and clairvoyant. She has worked with doctors, psychologists and scientists, which together with her psychic investigations has enabled her to bring out many unique facets concerning the healing of the psychological and physical aspects of man. She always approaches her work in a creative way, which leads to many new discoveries in the area she terms, "Holistic Spiritual Healing."

Gabriele Blackburn is the author of The Science and Art of the Pendulum, and has taught Radiesthesia and Healing seminars in the United States, Canada, and Europe to many health interested groups. Born in Europe, she has lived in India, and traveled extensively. She now resides in Ojai, California, and was married to the late Albert Blackburn, author of Now Consciousness and Worlds Beyond Thought.

- -

PLEASE SEND ME: THE LIGHT OF KRISHNAMURTI

Sorry - no phone orders.

Send check or money order
payable on any U.S. Bank *to:*

IDYLWILD BOOKS
P.O. Box 246, Ojai, CA 93024

Amount

How Many?_________ @ $14.00 each: _______
California Residents add 7¼% Sales Tax: _______
U.S. Mailing and Handling $2.50: _______
Foreign: $5.00 Surface Mail: _______
$15.00 Air Mail: _______
TOTAL ENCLOSED: _______

Order to be Sent to:

Name: ____

Address: ____

City: _____________________ State: __________ Zip: __________

THE SCIENCE AND ART OF THE PENDULUM:
A Complete Course in Radiesthesia

By Gabriele Blackburn

Published by:
IDYLWILD BOOKS
P.O. Box 246, Ojai, CA 93024
(805) 646-2646

Paperback 8½ x 11
96 Pages
ISBN: 0-9613054-1-X
© IDYLWILD BOOKS 1988

This course emphasizes the practical use of the pendulum in maintaining a state of health by determining the underlying causes of disease. The ancient art of the pendulum, now called Radiesthesia, or Psionic healing, opens many new fields of research, and when learned correctly can be an invaluable source of self-help. The proper use of the pendulum can determine many conditions in the body which no other tests will show, for example, the amount of pollution caused by our environment. The pendulum can guide one to lessen or eliminate states of imbalance, using natural, herbal or homeopathic remedies. With Radiesthesia the pendulist can determine the need for vitamins, minerals, and supplements on a daily basis; also which remedies and dosage to use when ill.

Through the author's psychic investigations into the conditions of the etheric body, she has developed new methods of using the pendulum. Insights into the principles of healing are pointed out in diagrams and shared. In this course she teaches the meaning, potential, and varied uses of color healing. Also included is how to test and treat each of the chakras, or nerve centers, for balancing the vital energy flow. The pendulist can measure predispositions, thereby having a unique tool to maintain a state of health. The mysterious art of "Broadcasting" healing remedies is also gone into very thoroughly. This course is both for the beginner, the professional healer, and anyone who is interested in broadening their understanding of healing, and the use of the pendulum.

Gabriele Blackburn is a spiritual healer and clairvoyant. She has worked with doctors, psychologists and scientists, which together with her psychic investigations has enabled her to bring out many unique facets concerning the healing of the psychological and physical aspects of man. She always approaches her work in a creative way, which leads to many new discoveries in the area she terms, "Holistic Spiritual Healing."

Gabriele Blackburn has taught Radiesthesia and Healing seminars in the United States, Canada, and Europe to many health interested groups. Born in Europe, she has lived in India, and traveled extensively. She now resides in Ojai, California, and was married to the late Albert Blackburn, author of Now Consciousness and Worlds Beyond Thought.

PLEASE SEND ME:

	Each	How Many?	Amount
The Book and All Materials Listed Below:	$40.00		
The Book Only:	$10.00		
Author's Pendulums:	$6.00		
Determination Boards and Pointers:	$6.00		
1 oz. Horseshoe Magnets:	$7.00		
Witness Folders: 50 Witnesses and Blood-Spot Envelopes:	$4.00		
15 Work-List Pages and 18 Anatomy Charts:	$7.00		

TOTAL ORDER:	
California Residents add 7¼% Sales Tax:	
U.S. Mailing and Handling $2.50:	
Foreign: $5.00 Surface Mail:	
$15.00 Air Mail:	
TOTAL ENCLOSED:	

> *Send check or money order* **payable on any U.S. Bank** *to:*
> **IDYLWILD BOOKS**
> P.O. Box 246, Ojai, CA 93024

Order to be Sent to:

Name: ____

Address: ____

City: _________________________ State: _____________ Zip: _____________

PROTECTING YOURSELF FROM ENERGY DEPLETION:
A Talk by Gabriele Blackburn

Author of
**THE
SCIENCE
AND ART
OF THE PENDULUM:**
A Complete Course in Radiesthesia

Produced by:
IDYLWILD BOOKS
P.O. Box 246, Ojai, CA 93024
(805) 646-2646

Audio Cassette:
Time: 1 Hour
© IDYLWILD BOOKS 1986

This tape is of vital importance to anyone involved in the healing arts, or working with the sick and dying, anyone overly sensitive to people, crowds, large cities, or in constant negative relationships. In order to stay healthy it is absolutely essential to know how to protect yourself from energy depletion, which affects you physically, emotionally, and mentally. How and why you may have opened yourself up to harmful outside influences, is gone into very thoroughly, and the many different ways in which you can protect yourself are carefully explained. You will learn what you can do yourself, but when it is necessary to seek help, where to find it.

On the second side of this tape are meditation-visualizations for general and specific protections. These include protections from illness, dangerous animals, anger and violence. Different ways are shown how you can be cleansed from negativity, which is picked up so easily. Also you are taught many effective ways to protect other people, your home, car, or an object. Furthermore, you will learn how to deal positively with negative people, environments and situations. Through these creative visualizations you will be able to increase your energy level and to live a healthier, safe life.

Gabriele Blackburn is a spiritual healer and clairvoyant. She has worked with doctors, psychologists and scientists, which together with her psychic investigations has enabled her to bring out many unique facets concerning the healing of the psychological and physical aspects of man. She always approaches her work in a creative way, which leads to many new discoveries in the area she terms, "Holistic Spiritual Healing."

Gabriele Blackburn has taught Radiesthesia and Healing seminars in the United States, Canada, and Europe to many health interested groups. Born in Europe, she has lived in India, and traveled extensively. She now resides in Ojai, California, and was married to the late Albert Blackburn, author of Now Consciousness and Worlds Beyond Thought.

PLEASE SEND ME:

Amount

PROTECTING YOURSELF FROM ENERGY DEPLETION

How Many?__________ @ $6.00 each: _______
California Residents add 7 1/4% Sales Tax: _______
U.S. Mailing and Handling $2.50: _______
Foreign: $5.00 Surface Mail: _______
$15.00 Air Mail: _______
TOTAL ENCLOSED: _______

*ALL TAPES
WARRANTED
AGAINST
DEFECTS*

Send check or money order **payable on any U.S. Bank** to:

IDYLWILD BOOKS
P.O. Box 246, Ojai, CA 93024

Order to be Sent to:

Name: ____

Address: ____

City: _________________________________ State: ___________ Zip: ___________

SONGS OF LIGHT

Five Original Songs
Created in moments of intuition and sung

by

Gabriele Blackburn

As If With You

Keep Moving

Stupid Old Me

Thinking Of You

Meditation Is To See

AUDIO CASSETTE   20 Minutes

$5.00

No mailing cost if included with any order

Create-Your-Own
Perpetual Calendar®

Easy to use — Never out of date

Use 12 of your own photos or pictures

Create a treasured keepsake – a unique gift

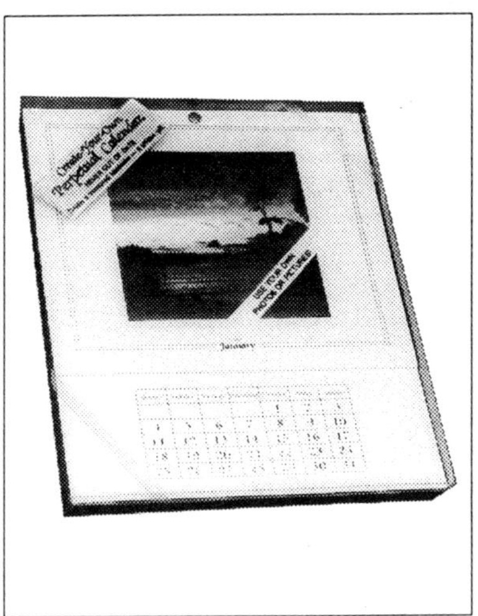

=== A WALL HANGING CALENDAR ===

By simply using appropriate month & date cards, this perpetual calendar will never be out of date.

Will fit standard 8 x 10 or 10 x 12 frame

AN EXCITING __NEW__ IDEA IN CALENDARS!
ARTISTICALLY PRODUCED!!
A UNIQUE CONVERSATION PIECE!!!

You'll Love It!!!

Published by:
IDYLWILD BOOKS
P.O. Box 246, Ojai, CA 93024
(805) 646-2646

Month & Date Cards
Size: 8 x 10
Packaged in See-Thru Boxes
ISBN: 0-9613054-2-8
© IDYLWILD BOOKS 1986

Please send me: *Create-Your-Own*
Perpetual Calendar®

	Amount
Send check or money order **payable on any U.S. Bank** to:	
IDYLWILD BOOKS P.O. Box 246, Ojai, CA 93024	

How Many?_________ @ $9.00 each: _________
California Residents add 7¼% Sales Tax: _________
U.S. Mailing and Handling $2.50: _________
Foreign: $5.00 Surface Mail: _________
$15.00 Air Mail: _________
TOTAL ENCLOSED: _________

Order to be Sent to:

Name: ____

Address: ____

City: _________________________ State: _________ Zip: _________

NOW CONSCIOUSNESS:
Exploring the World Beyond Thought
By Albert Blackburn

Published by:
IDYLWILD BOOKS
P.O. Box 246, Ojai, CA 93024
(805) 646-2646

Paperback 5³/₈ x 8³/₈
176 Pages
ISBN: 0-9613054-0-1
© IDYLWILD BOOKS 1983

The intimate contemporary account of one man's quest is a valuable step-by-step approach that anyone can follow on the path of self-knowledge. During an interview with J. Krishnamurti in 1944 the author underwent a radical inner transformation, a turning about at the deepest seat of consciousness. The result: Now Consciousness, the perception of reality moment-to-moment, free of time and discrimination. This awareness leads to an inner clarity that enables the individual to objectively watch the intricacies of the thought process and explore the secrets of consciousness.

Albert Blackburn's straightforward accounting of his own experiences make this work ideal for anyone interested in the dynamics of consciousness and the psychology of transpersonal experiencing. The author disputes the necessity of a linear approach to enlightenment; instead he suggests the possibility of a vertical, instantaneous breakthrough, free of time.

Albert Blackburn was born in Cincinnati, Ohio in 1910. He began a career in aviation in 1928 after graduating from the first approved flying school in the U.S. This led to barnstorming, flight instruction, and eventually to airport ownership and flight school operations from 1938 to 1950. Wishing to give all of his time to his inward exploration of consciousness, he gave up his airport business and moved to Ojai, California. Mr. Blackburn was a member of the Theosophical Society from 1934 to 1944, was associated with the Happy Valley School from 1948 to 1958, and Krishnamurti Writings Inc. from 1946 to 1966; he was also briefly associated with the Krishnamurti Foundation of America. Since 1974 he has been teaching, writing, and giving talks in various places in the U.S. and Canada, utilizing his own experiences and understanding of life.

Now Consciousness: *Exploring the World Beyond Thought is a stimulating and perceptive account of Albert Blackburn's/the author's experience in transpersonal realms. The personal account of his time with Krishnamurti is especially interesting, and his treatment of the process of self-realization is – to use a word the author may regard as inappropriate – thoughtful.*

John White
Author of *"Frontiers of Consciousness"*

PLEASE SEND ME: **NOW CONSCIOUSNESS**

Send check or money order **payable on any U.S. Bank** *to:*

IDYLWILD BOOKS
P.O. Box 246, Ojai, CA 93024

Amount

How Many?_________ @ \$8.95 each: _______
California Residents add 7¹/₄% Sales Tax: _______
U.S. Mailing and Handling \$2.50: _______
Foreign: \$5.00 Surface Mail: _______
\$15.00 Air Mail: _______
TOTAL ENCLOSED: _______

Order to be Sent to:

Name: ____

Address: ____

City: ___________________________ State: ___________ Zip: ___________

FURTHER EXPLORATION INTO NOW CONSCIOUSNESS:
Discussions with Albert Blackburn

Author of **NOW CONSCIOUSNESS**

Produced by:
IDYLWILD BOOKS
P.O. Box 246, Ojai, CA 93024
(805) 646-2646

Audio Cassette:
Time: 1 Hour each
© IDYLWILD BOOKS 1986

We invite you to participate in this exciting exploration into the world beyond thought. In these tapes Albert Blackburn, with his wife Gabriele, discuss his creative and completely extemporaneous, step-by-step exploration into insight. Using the words as a mirror, the listener can be led imperceptively into an actual experiencing of what is being discussed. True listening, in which there is no judgment, evaluation or a retreat into a preconceived idea, invites holistic understanding at the level where inner transformation can occur.

#1 An Introduction to Now Consciousness

Covers: A comparison between occultism, mysticism and now consciousness. Do all paths lead to the ultimate Truth? Experiencing reality beyond psychological time. The results of 'meditation.' What is a religious life?

#2 Direct Perception

Covers: The ending of psychological time. The possible effect of computerized living on brain development. The possibility of by-passing conditioning through direct perception.

#3 Experiencing

Covers: The fundamental difference between an experience and experiencing. How experiences are routed through the brain into the content of consciousness. Experiencing the completeness of each moment opens the door to insight and self-discovery. With insight we can live intelligently.

#4 The Quiet Mind

Covers: Can the manipulation of thought, through meditation lead to a quiet mind? What is real stillness? How true stillness can come into being with no effort. The ending of the psychological 'me,' and the discovery of reality moment-to-moment.

#5 Exploring the World Beyond Thought

Covers: What is the origin of thinking? Two kinds of memory. Insight – direct action – faith. The difference between knowledge and knowing. Can one live without psychological time?

#6 Enlightenment

Covers: The real meaning and results of enlightenment: freedom from the known, use of a different energy, no conflict, no fear, order, integrity, understanding, faith, harmlessness, honesty and inner peace.

#7 Holistic Understanding

Covers: Four levels of understanding. Integrated understanding on all levels is the beginning of an entirely new way of living. Is suffering an intrinsic part of the evolutionary process? How to completely eliminate psychological suffering. What is spiritual alchemy?

		Each	How Many?	Amount
PLEASE SEND ME:	#1 Introduction to Now Consciousness	$6.00		
	#2 Direct Perception	$6.00		
ALL TAPES	#3 Experiencing	$6.00		
WARRANTED	#4 The Quiet Mind	$6.00		
AGAINST	#5 Exploring the World Beyond Thought	$6.00		
DEFECTS	#6 Enlightenment	$6.00		
	#7 Holistic Understanding	$6.00		

TOTAL ORDER: _______
California Residents add 7¼% Sales Tax: _______
U.S. Mailing and Handling $2.50: _______
Foreign: $5.00 Surface Mail: _______
$15.00 Air Mail: _______
TOTAL ENCLOSED: _______

*Send check or money order **payable on any U.S. Bank** to:*
IDYLWILD BOOKS
P.O. Box 246, Ojai, CA 93024

Order to be Sent to:

Name: ____

Address: ____

City: _________________ State: _____________ Zip: _____________

WORLDS BEYOND THOUGHT:

Conversations on Now Consciousness

By Albert Blackburn

Published by:
IDYLWILD BOOKS
P.O. Box 246, Ojai, CA 93024
(805) 646-2646

Paperback 5³/₈ x 8³/₈
218 Pages
ISBN: 0-9613054-3-6
© IDYLWILD BOOKS 1988

In *WORLDS BEYOND THOUGHT* Albert Blackburn guides the reader to an understanding of what it means to live moment by moment, free of the insidious thought process that causes all of our psychological problems. He emphasizes the importance of a complete awareness of the present moment, a holistic perception that can bring about a quiet mind, clarity, and order in one's life, and lead to an experiencing of that which is beyond human consciousness, which is sacred, all Love and Light.

The seven conversations that comprise the major part of *WORLDS BEYOND THOUGHT* are revised and expanded versions of actual dialogues between Albert Blackburn and his wife, Gabriele. Before his death in June, 1987, he spent months carefully editing the transcripts of these conversations, expanding and clarifying his ideas, and making certain that necessary changes did not modify or distort his meaning in any way. These thoughtful elucidations make *WORLDS BEYOND THOUGHT* a valuable study in self-realization, and the author's revolutionary insights may help others to resolve their own fundamental problems. Some of Mr. Blackburn's letters, which he felt contained a unique approach to discovering answers to the many basic questions of life, have been included with the dialogues to give the book an additional dimension.

Albert Blackburn was a close friend of J. Krishnamurti, whose teachings inspired the radical inner transformation that the author described in his previous book, NOW CONSCIOUSNESS. *Mr. Blackburn lived his life with great intensity, motivated solely by the desire to be totally free of ego, self-will, and need for personal gratification. His serious investigations into the meaning of life were expressed with a clarity that characterized everything that he wrote or spoke, every word of which originated in his own holistic understanding of life. His inner commitment brought him into extensive contact with people from many countries and many walks of life, all of whom were enriched by the deep insights that characterized his approach to living.*

- -

PLEASE SEND ME: **WORLDS BEYOND THOUGHT**

Send check or money order **payable on any U.S. Bank** *to:* **IDYLWILD BOOKS** P.O. Box 246, Ojai, CA 93024	**Amount** **How Many?**________ @ **$12.00 each:** ________ California Residents add 7¹/₄% Sales Tax: ________ U.S. Mailing and Handling $2.50: ________ Foreign: $5.00 Surface Mail: ________ $15.00 Air Mail: ________ **TOTAL ENCLOSED:** ________

Order to be Sent to:

Name: ____

Address: ____

City: __________________________________ State: _____________ Zip: _____________